THE
COMPLETE
WEDDING
PLANNER

The Diagram Group

Editor	Denis Kennedy
Editorial staff	Susan Bosanko, David Harding
Design director	Philip Patenall
Design staff	Suzanne Baker, Richard Czapnik, Brian Hewson, Alastair Burnside, Joe Bonello, Paula Preston
Illustrator	Anna Kostal

First published 1986 by
William Collins Sons & Co. Ltd

Reprinted 1988, 1989, 1990, 1992, 1993

British Library Cataloguing in Publication Data
The Complete wedding planner.
　1. Weddings
　395'22　　HQ745

ISBN 0-00-412031-0

Printed and bound in Great Britain
by HarperCollins Manufacturing, Glasgow

THE COMPLETE WEDDING PLANNER

Gail Lawther

HarperCollins*Publishers*

Contents

Foreword

So – the two of you are about to take one of the biggest steps of your life and get married. Congratulations! *The Complete Wedding Planner* is just the book you have been looking for to help you through the maze of engagement and marriage preparations.

Engagement and marriage require an enormous amount of thinking and planning for bride and groom; this book has been prepared to make the task easier and more enjoyable for both of you. Of course, some duties belong exclusively to the husband-to-be and some to the prospective bride, but more and more couples these days are doing the planning and preparation together. Read through these pages as a couple; the hints, checklists and timetables will help you to ensure that everything is done in good time for the wedding, and that your big day fulfils all your hopes for it.

There are so many things to get done, but with the help of *The Complete Wedding Planner* the preparations shouldn't be a chore, but a chance to work together in preparation for being husband and wife. Enjoy yourselves!

Rings

Engagement rings

One of the first things that almost every engaged couple does is to buy a ring for the girl to wear on her ring finger. The giving of a ring for a betrothal is a very ancient custom; the Romans used to give a ring to seal a marriage bargain. Generally it is only the girl who wears an engagement ring, but some men like to wear a signet ring during this time, while others choose to wear their wedding ring on the third finger of the right hand, and transfer it at the marriage ceremony. However, you can be sure that as soon as you say you are engaged people will ask to see your ring, and in fact it may prove to be the most special and the most expensive piece of jewellery you will ever buy, so take your time choosing exactly what you want.

Diamonds

A diamond solitaire has been the traditional ring in recent years. This is partly because the rarity of diamonds makes them much sought after, and also because the durability of the stones mean that they really are quite likely to last 'forever'. Good quality diamonds are expensive, and are not a particularly good investment because of the mark-up you have to pay on the initial purchase, so only choose a diamond ring if you want it for its intrinsic beauty or symbolic value.

When choosing a diamond, remember the four C's: carat, cut, clarity and colour. Carat is the weight of the diamond, cut is the shape into which it has been carved to increase its sparkle, clarity is its freedom from major flaws and colour is its whiteness. These things can be hard for an amateur to judge, so it is worth getting advice from someone you trust. If you want the appearance of a diamond without the expense, cubic zirconium makes a very good imitation diamond at a fraction of the price.

Other options

Diamonds are by no means the only choice for engagement rings. Any other precious or semi-precious stones may be used, or you could have a ring specially modelled from gold or platinum that has been moulded, carved, faceted or decorated with flowers, symbols, punched holes, initials, etc. You could go for a single stone such as an opal or a sapphire, in a plain or elaborate setting, or a cluster of stones either mixed or all the same. Stones can be solitaire, set in bands, set in a regular grouping such as a circle, an oval, a heart or a square, or set asymmetrically for a modern look. In order to make your ring extra personal, you chould choose your birthstone, a significant combination of stones, or a special design such as a flower.

Rings are used for betrothal or marriage in many cultures – but not always on the finger! In Zaire women marrying important men of the tribe have large gold rings welded around their ankles, and have to wear them always. Although this must be cumbersome – the rings can weigh up to 7 Kg (15lb) – it has its benefits, as it also means that the woman is exempted from any heavy work for the rest of her life.

Stone cuts

Precious stones (diamonds, emeralds, sapphires and rubies) are cut into multi-faceted shapes that increase their internal 'fire' or sparkle. This is also done with some hard semi-precious stones such as amethyst, beryl, zircon and tourmaline. Softer stones, or stones with no internal fire, such as coral, opal, lapis lazuli, tiger's eye, agate and bloodstone are cut into a smooth shape known as a cabochon. Different cuts suit different stones as they capitalise on the stone's internal structure. The common cuts are shown here from the top and from the side.

1 Cabochon cut
2 Baguette cut, particularly suitable for emeralds and sapphires.
3 Rose cut, a cut that leaves numerous triangular surfaces.
4 Trap cut, a simple squared-off cut.
5 Antique cushion, a fancy cut for rectangular stones.
6 Brilliant cut, the most common cut used for diamonds.
7 Fancy cut, used to facet a pear-shaped stone.

The language of rings

This traditional language of rings applies to both men and women.
Ring on the first finger of the left hand: I want to be married.
Ring on the second finger: I prefer platonic friendship.
Ring on the third finger: I am engaged or married.
Ring on the little finger: I never intend to marry.

Rings – Stones/Motto rings

Precious and semi-precious stones

There are numerous stones to choose from for your engagement ring, and they come in a wide variety of colours. The only true precious stones are diamonds, rubies, emeralds and sapphires; all the others are known as semi-precious or ornamental stones.

Stone	Colour
Agate	*banded in different colours*
Amethyst	*purple*
Aquamarine	*pale blue-green*
Beryl (citrine)	*yellow*
Bloodstone	*green with red flecks*
Cameo	*white image carved out of pink shell*
Cornelian	*orange*
Chalcedony	*white*
Chrysoberyl	*darkish green*
Coral	*generally orange, can be red or white*
Garnet	*purple-red*
Jade	*generally green, can be yellow, pink or white*
Jasper	*brown with coloured flecks*
Jet	*black*
Lapis lazuli	*blue with gold flecks*
Malachite	*banded green*
Moonstone	*translucent white*
Obsidian	*black*
Onyx	*banded black*
Opal	*white, red or turquoise with rainbow flecks*
Pearl	*white or pale pink*
Rhodonite	*pale pink*
Rose quartz	*pink*
Spinel	*generally red, can be brown, green or blue*
Tiger's eye	*banded brown*
Topaz	*yellow, brown or pink*
Tourmaline	*generally blue or pink, can be red, brown or green*
Zircon	*pale blue*

Month stones

Certain gemstones are associated with different months; you might like to choose a ring that uses stones from the month of your birth. Each of the month stones is supposed to symbolise one or more qualities.

January	Garnet	*Constancy*
February	Amethyst	*Sincerity*
March	Bloodstone	*Courage*
April	Diamond	*Innocence or lasting love*
May	Emerald	*Success or hope*
June	Pearl	*Health or purity*
July	Ruby	*Love and contentment*
August	Sardonyx	*Married happiness*
September	Sapphire	*Wisdom or repentance*
October	Opal	*Hope*
November	Topaz	*Fidelity or cheerfulness*
December	Turquoise	*Harmony*

Motto rings

Motto rings were very common in Victorian times, when overt expressions of sentiment were encouraged! The idea is to spell out the name of the loved one, or a suitable sentiment, using the initial letters of the gemstones in the ring. Of course this idea is limited by the initials available from desirable gemstones, but it is a rather pretty custom you might like to try and imitate if your name, or his, is suitable – or you could use gemstones that represent your two sets of initials.

DEAREST – *diamond, emerald, amethyst, ruby, emerald, sapphire, topaz*
REGARD – *ruby, emerald, garnet, amethyst, ruby, diamond*
PETER – *pearl, emerald, topaz, emerald, ruby*
GEORGE – *garnet, emerald, opal, ruby, garnet, emerald*
ROBERT – *ruby, opal, beryl, emerald, ruby, tourmaline*
SARA – *sapphire, amethyst, ruby, amethyst*
DEBRA – *diamond, emerald, beryl, ruby, amethyst*
CAROL – *coral, amethyst, ruby, opal, lapis lazuli*
ZOE – *zircon, opal, emerald*
PAM – *pearl, amethyst, moonstone*

Rings – Ring finger/Styles/Checklist

Ring finger

Why is the fourth finger (counting the thumb) of the left hand the finger for engagement and wedding rings? The ancient philosophers asserted that there was a very delicate nerve running from that finger direct to the heart; later writers said that it was a fine vein, the *vena amoris*. In Catholic tradition the first three fingers represent the Trinity, so their ring-giving ceremony consists of putting the ring on the thumb, forefinger and third finger while saying 'In the name of the Father, Son and Holy Ghost', and then on the fourth finger, to rest permanently, while saying 'Amen'. Up until the 16th century it was the custom here and elsewhere to wear the betrothal or wedding ring on the fourth finger of the right hand, a custom that is still echoed when nuns take their vows.

Wedding rings

In some cultures it is the custom for engaged couples to exchange identical plain gold bands that are later used for the wedding service, but in this country it is more customary to buy separate rings as wedding rings. The wedding ring is round to represent eternity, and for this reason it is supposed to be completely plain, or to have the same design running all the way around its surface. The gold represents preciousness, as it is one of the most highly valued metals in all cultures (in ancient Rome only a few important people had what was known as the *jus annuli aurei*, the right to wear a gold ring). These days some couples choose platinum, as it is even more expensive than gold. Gold is also measured in carats (not the same as the carats used for diamonds); in this case it is a measure of purity. 24-carat gold is the purest, but is too soft to use for everyday wear, so the best gold generally available is 18-carat. 9-carat gold has a higher proportion of other metals and is harder, lighter in colour, and cheaper. If you buy your engagement ring and wedding ring separately, check that they are the same carat or else one will rub away at the other.

Styles of wedding ring

Wedding rings can be bought in a wide variety of finishes – smooth, flat bands, faceted, carved, engraved, moulded into fancy shapes or decorated with other metals. It is also possible to buy matching wedding and engagement rings in many styles, and men's and women's versions of the same style of ring.

Checkpoints for buying an engagement ring

What kind of stones do I want?
Do I want a solitaire, or a cluster of stones, or a band?
Do I want anything unusual, in style, stones or setting? If so, am I likely to find it in the shops or should we have it made?
How much can we afford to spend?
Will I still be happy with this ring in several years' time?
Are the stones good quality and regular in shape and colour?
Are there any rough edges on the stones or settings?
If I want something costly, could I buy it second-hand?
Will the ring be easy to keep clean and sparkling?

Checkpoints for buying a wedding ring

Are we going to have two rings at the service or just one?
Do we want matching rings?
Do I want a ring to match my engagement ring?
Does this ring go with my engagement ring, in looks and fit?
How much can we afford to spend?
Does the ring need altering – if so, is this included in the cost or is it extra?
Do we want anything engraved on the ring(s)?
Do we want a pouch or case to keep the ring(s) in until the ceremony?

When you have made up your mind about your engagement ring or wedding rings, remember to ask the jeweller for a valuation certificate for insurance purposes, and also to ask his advice on caring for your ring (particularly cleaning), keeping it away from certain substances, etc.

Announcing your engagement

Sharing your news

The first thing that you want to do when you are engaged is – tell everyone!
And, of course, all your family and friends will want to share in the good news
and to wish you well. Announcing an engagement is a much less formal event
these days than it used to be, but it is still worth following a few basic
guidelines to make sure that everyone hears the news and that nothing is left
out.

$$* * *$$

Telling parents

The days are past when a young man had to have a formal interview with his
prospective father-in-law to ask him for his daughter's hand in marriage; these
days an engagement is almost exclusively a matter for a couple to decide for
themselves. However, a wise man will try to make sure that he is on good
terms with his fiancée's parents, that they have no absolute objection to the
marriage, and that they are satisfied that he has a good chance of making their
daughter happy and providing a stable marriage, both emotionally and
financially.

It is traditional to tell the bride's parents first, ideally on a visit from both
partners. If you cannot tell them in person, a phone call is the next best
solution. Try not to write with the news unless you live impossibly far away
from your family. The next people to be told are the groom's parents, again in
person or by telephone. These days most people are already well acquainted
with their future parents-in-law before the engagement is announced, but
there are exceptions especially if the couple has met at college or abroad. If
you are already engaged before you meet your fiancé(e)s parents, remember
that they are probably feeling just as nervous as you are! Try to be relaxed,
and you will have the best chance of starting a pleasant relationship that will
stand you in good stead in later years.

Telling families

It is really up to you how you tell the other members of your families, and will
probably depend on how close you are geographically and emotionally. Some
people will appreciate a visit from you and your partner; others will be happy
with a phone call, and still others will be quite satisfied with a letter. However,
make sure that you try to tell them all roughly at the same time, so that no-one
is offended.

Telling friends

Your friends may well have guessed at your engagement before you tell them officially. Once again, try to make sure that everyone is told at roughly the same time, and don't leave anyone out. This is rarely a problem as most newly-engaged couples are only too happy to spend an afternoon on the phone ringing round with the good news.

Announcing at a party

You may wish to announce your engagement as a surprise at a party. Traditionally this should be a party given by the girl's parents who, along with the man's parents, should already be in the know. Her mother issues the invitations – keeping the purpose of the party a secret – and then the official announcement can be made by her father or by her fiancé. Other couples prefer to have a party for their friends and announce the engagement to them, having already told both sets of parents. Usually the engagement ring is not worn in public until the engagement has been officiallly announced.

Parents' duties

As soon as possible after the engagement has been announced, it is customary for the two sets of parents to try to meet. This could be arranged by the couple themselves, or one set of parents can act as host and hostess to the other. Of course this may not be possible if they live at some distance from one another, so in this case it is a nice gesture if they exchange letters mentioning how happy they are for the couple concerned, and that they are looking forward to meeting one another at the wedding.

Keeping quiet

It would be in very bad taste to announce your intention to marry someone else if you were still in the middle of incomplete divorce or annulment proceedings – or, even worse, if you had not yet started them. Wait until you are both fully free to marry before making any announcement.

In Jewish tradition, marriage is thought to be the ideal state, and so an engagement is the cause of great rejoicing. The first blessing said over a baby is that he or she will one day be a radiant groom or bride.

*

In Germany, couples usually exchange plain, identical rings as a token of engagement, and these are later used as their wedding rings.

Announcing your engagement – Newspapers/Checklist

Newspaper announcements

You may wish to have your engagement announced in the local or national newspapers, either as a way of telling all and sundry or as a special way of marking the event. The traditional way of making the announcement is for the bride's mother to take responsibility, and so formal announcements tend to depend on her present status for their wording.

The correct formal wording is:
Mr and Mrs George Davidson are pleased to announce the engagement of their daughter Jane to Mr John Smith, son of Mr and Mrs Alan Smith of Newport, Isle of Wight.

Or, alternatively:
The engagement is announced between Jane, daughter of Mr and Mrs George Davidson of Westminster, and Mr John Smith, son of Mr and Mrs Alan Smith of Newport, Isle of Wight.

A less formal version could be:
George and Jean Davidson are delighted to announce the engagement of their daughter Jane to John, son of Alan and Elizabeth Smith of Newport.

If the girl's parents are separated or divorced the engagement could be worded:
The engagement is announced between Jane, daughter of Mrs Jean Davidson (or Mrs Jean Watson if she has remarried) and Mr George Davidson, and John...etc.

Many other variations are possible in formal announcements if the girl is adopted, a stepdaughter, a niece, fostered, etc. Just remember that there is no need to get tied up with formalities – a simple statement of fact, and of the relationship, is much the best.

These days many couples prefer to announce their engagement themselves, whether it is a first or second marriage. In this case the announcement can be formal or informal, with the bride's or the groom's name coming first, and with or without the date of the wedding. The main thing to remember with all newspaper announcements is that the copy may be needed up to four weeks before publication.

Checklist for announcing your engagement

Use this list to make sure that you tell all of you family and friends that you are engaged, noting whether you are going to tell them by visit, phone call, or letter.

Name	Method	Name	Method

Preparing for marriage

Thinking ahead

What are your expectations of marriage? Or haven't you thought that far? It may be that you are caught up with the mechanics of your actual wedding day, and it may be difficult to look beyond that to your marriage itself. But remember that your wedding day should only be the start; it is the marriage itself that will take the time, the effort, the planning. You are two very different people coming together to live permanently under the same roof, and it is unrealistic to expect that everything will fall perfectly into place immediately the register is signed.

It is well worth taking the time now, during your engagement, to look ahead to your marriage and to try and sidestep some of the common pitfalls. Obviously at the moment everything is rosy and full of promise, but with the best will in the world it won't always be like that. Even the very happiest marriages have their times of stress, of illness, of feeling low, of wondering whether you actually are the right partners for each other. Use your engagement to talk through as many issues as you can think of that might crop up during your marriage; try and imagine difficult situations, and how you would cope in them.

Communication is the key to a successful and happy marriage – but don't expect it to arrive out of thin air as soon as the knot is tied! Good communication is built up slowly, and your engagement is the ideal time to start building, while you are involved but before the full pressures of marriage are upon you. Learn to talk to one another honestly, without anger or recriminations; learn to talk things through if you have a problem, rather than hoping that it will go away. Look together at your attitudes to the various aspects of your marriage and see whether you agree or disagree.

If you are getting married in church, the minister might suggest that you attend a course of marriage preparation classes. Do attend if you are offered that chance – thinking through some of the issues involved before the wedding can help keep marriages out of the divorce courts. The classes will also help you to understand the vows that you will be taking in church, and the way that the church sees the marriage bond.

Talking it through

Take the opportunity of your engagement to talk and think through some of the issues surrounding marriage. The points mentioned here may well be important at some stage or another in your married life and it is worth sorting out your views while you are not under pressure. Talk them through together and compare notes – you might be surprised at each other's answers! – and also think them through on your own, trying to be honest about your own and your partner's strengths and failings.

Each other

What do I expect from my marriage?
Are my expectations of my partner realistic?
What will I be able to give to this marriage?
Am I willing to work at the relationship?
What are my strong points?
How can these be used in our marriage?
What are my weak points?
How might these be a danger to the relationship?
What can I do about them?
Does my partner realise them?
What are my partner's strong and weak points?
How do I feel about them in relation to our marriage?
Do I have any reservations about our marriage?
If so, what are they? Are they serious?
How can these reservations be overcome?
How will I feel if my partner seems to stop trying in the relationship?
Is the strength of my love as strong as my partner's?
If not, will this be a problem?
Do I really mean 'for better, for worse'?
How would I feel if my partner became ill?
Would my partner support me if I became ill?
Do we communicate well?
Do we argue?
How do we handle disagreements?
Do we find it hard to make up after disagreements?
How can we improve our communication?
Is there anything about my partner that could become irritating?
If so, what can I do about it?
Am I expecting to change my partner's character or habits?
Am I expecting to change my own character or habits?

Preparing for marriage – Thinking and talking it through

Family

Do I get on with my partner's parents and family?
Does my partner get on with my parents and family?
Are there any areas of friction?
If so, what can we do about them?
Do we come from similar social backgrounds?
If not, is this a problem? Or could it become one?
Do we have similar attitudes to family get-togethers?
Is either of us too dependent on our own family?
How often will we expect to see our families after our marriage?
How often will they expect to see us?
Will I be tempted to put my family before my marriage?
Are our family situations similar or different? (For instance, the number of children in the family, attitudes to money, etc.)
If so, is this going to be a problem?

Money

Do we have similar attitudes to spending money?
What are our attitudes to saving?
What are our attitudes to giving money to charity, church, needy causes?
Do we like entertaining?
How often will we want to entertain?
Will we have to entertain as part of our jobs?
How much of our money should go on our home?
What kind of holidays do we want to save for?
Does either of us find it difficult to hold on to money?
Does either of us find it difficult to let go of money?
Have we ever encountered problems over money?
Do we think we are ever likely to?
How do we both feel about buying on credit?
How would we cope with redundancy, disability, or anything else that affected our income?
If we have children, are we prepared for a drop in spending money?

'When people are tied up for life, 'tis in their mutual interest not to grow weary of one another.'

Lady Mary Wortley Montague

Leisure

How do we like to spend our spare time?
Do we have many interests in common?
Are there any interests that the other partner dislikes?
Is this likely to become a problem?
Do I resent any of my partner's pastimes?
Do we want to spend all our leisure time together?
Do we share the same friends?
Does my partner dislike any of my friends?
Do I dislike any of my partner's friends?
If so, what are we going to do about it?

Sex

What are our expectations of sex in our marriage?
Do we have a similar sex drive?
Are we going to keep our marriage exclusive?
Do we have similar sexual backgrounds?
Do I find it difficult to talk about sex?
Does my partner find it difficult to talk about sex?
How would we cope with sexual difficulties?
What are our attitudes to contraception?
What form of contraception do we want to use?

Children

Do I want children?
Does my partner want children?
If we disagree, how are we going to resolve the problem?
If we do want children, how many?
When would we want our first child?
How would we cope with an unexpected pregnancy?
How will we feel if we can't have children?
What changes will children bring to our marriage?
Are we prepared to cope with those changes?

Preparing for marriage – The rules of love

The art of love

During the 12th century one Andreas Capellanus ('Andrew the Chaplain') wrote a treatise in Latin called the *Art of Loving*. In it he laid down 31 rules of love; no-one is quite sure whether they were to be taken seriously or whether they were tongue-in-cheek! However, here they are.

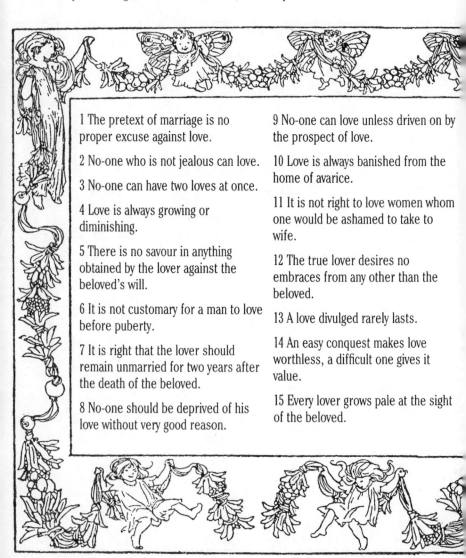

1 The pretext of marriage is no proper excuse against love.

2 No-one who is not jealous can love.

3 No-one can have two loves at once.

4 Love is always growing or diminishing.

5 There is no savour in anything obtained by the lover against the beloved's will.

6 It is not customary for a man to love before puberty.

7 It is right that the lover should remain unmarried for two years after the death of the beloved.

8 No-one should be deprived of his love without very good reason.

9 No-one can love unless driven on by the prospect of love.

10 Love is always banished from the home of avarice.

11 It is not right to love women whom one would be ashamed to take to wife.

12 The true lover desires no embraces from any other than the beloved.

13 A love divulged rarely lasts.

14 An easy conquest makes love worthless, a difficult one gives it value.

15 Every lover grows pale at the sight of the beloved.

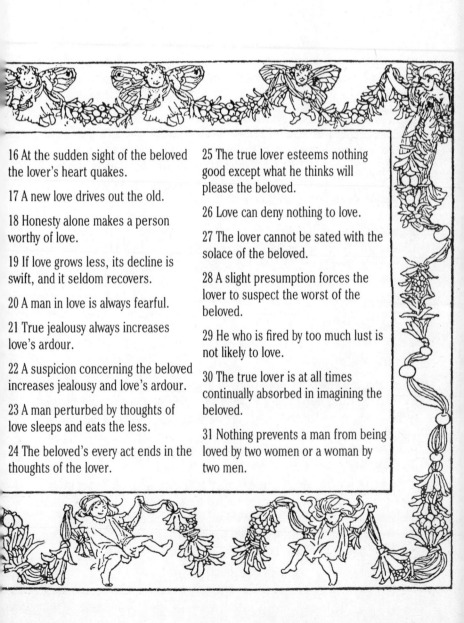

16 At the sudden sight of the beloved the lover's heart quakes.

17 A new love drives out the old.

18 Honesty alone makes a person worthy of love.

19 If love grows less, its decline is swift, and it seldom recovers.

20 A man in love is always fearful.

21 True jealousy always increases love's ardour.

22 A suspicion concerning the beloved increases jealousy and love's ardour.

23 A man perturbed by thoughts of love sleeps and eats the less.

24 The beloved's every act ends in the thoughts of the lover.

25 The true lover esteems nothing good except what he thinks will please the beloved.

26 Love can deny nothing to love.

27 The lover cannot be sated with the solace of the beloved.

28 A slight presumption forces the lover to suspect the worst of the beloved.

29 He who is fired by too much lust is not likely to love.

30 The true lover is at all times continually absorbed in imagining the beloved.

31 Nothing prevents a man from being loved by two women or a woman by two men.

Marriage and the law

Legal requirements

Who may marry whom is an issue that is important in most civilisations the world over. Some traditions are keen to keep the purity of the race unsullied; in these cases it may be illegal, or unpopular, to marry someone outside your own tribe, race, caste or even family. We can see the legacy of this idea in royal marriages; in most countries with royal families there is a restriction on whom the monarch or heir to the throne may or may not marry. In other traditions the laws are concerned with preventing inbreeding, and in these cases it is illegal to marry someone who is closely related. These are called the laws of consanguinity.

In England in the 14th century the laws of consanguinity were so complex that it was a veritable minefield trying to find someone that you *could* marry. A widow or widower could not marry the first, second or even third cousin of a deceased spouse, and godparents were also looked upon as blood relations; two people who had been godparents to the same child were not allowed to marry. As a result of the constant confusion over who was related to whom, the system of calling the banns was introduced in the 14th century; the names of the two people intending to marry had to be read aloud for three consecutive Sundays before the wedding. Presumably this gave the congregation the best part of a month to work out whether there was any relationship or not!

England and Wales

The current requirements in England and Wales allow for eight different ways of getting married legally.

Following the rites of the Church of England

1 By publication of banns. The banns are published by being read aloud on three successive Sundays before the wedding, often the three Sundays just before. If the couple live in the same parish the banns are read in the parish church where they will be married; if they live in separate parishes they are read in both parishes. If the person is generally known by a name other than the one on his or her birth certificate, then the banns are published in his or her popular name, or in both that name and the name on the certificate. Once the banns have been published the wedding can take place at any time within the three following months. If the wedding has to be delayed beyond this time the banns have to be published again.

2 By common licence. Common licences make the reading of the banns unnecessary and only one clear day's notice is required before the licence is issued. They are available from the Bishop's registered office in every cathedral town and from certain other authorised personnel. If you want a common licence the minister of the church will tell you where to apply. One of the partners has to apply in person and sign a declaration that there is no legal reason why they cannot marry, and that one or other partner, or both, has lived for at least 15 days in the area served by the church where the marriage is to be held.

3 By special licence. Special licences are issued only by the Archbishop of Canterbury, and only if there is some very urgent reason why the normal reading of the banns cannot take place. A special licence allows the wedding to take place at any time and in any place within the following three months.

4 By Superintendent Registrar's certificate. This is a certificate issued by a registrar allowing a Church of England minister to conduct a marriage, but is a method that is very rarely used.

Before a registrar

1 By Superintendent Registrar's certificate. A form is completed stating the names of the partners, their addresses and ages, the name of the building to be used for the wedding, and a signed declaration that there is no legal objection to the marriage. Both partners must have lived in the area for seven days prior to the declaration, or each must make a separate declaration before the registrar of their own district.

2 By certificate and licence. In this case only one partner needs to make a declaration, but the other must either be within England or Wales or have his or her usual residence there.

3 By Registrar General's licence. This is reserved for cases of extreme illness when it would be impossible to marry anywhere other than in hospital or at the sick person's home.

In churches of other denominations

In these cases the authorised registrar for the area concerned grants a licence. The church or building where the wedding is to take place should normally be licenced for marriages, and the registrar or other authorised person – usually the minister – must be there to register the marriage.

Marriage and the law – Locations

Scotland

Gretna Green has over the years acquired an aura associating it with runaway marriages and elopements, as it is the first place over the Scottish border and Scotland's regulations on marriage are not as restrictive as those of England and Wales. Scotland was outside the scope of the 1754 Marriage Act that governed the other countries; at one time it was possible to marry in Scotland simply by a declaration before two witnesses, but their laws have now been tightened up considerably and are bound by the Marriage (Scotland) Act of 1977.

You may marry in Scotland provided that you are 16 or over; if you are under 18 you do not need to have the permission of your parents or guardian. You can be married by a registrar or assistant registrar in the registry office, or you can be married by any clergyman, parson, priest or officer of any religious denomination who is entitled to undertake marriages according to the 1977 Act. Whichever type of wedding you choose, you must have two witnesses present who are over 16. Banns are not necessary for Scottish church weddings, and the minister has wider discretionary powers than he does in England and Wales; for instance, he may be willing to marry you in your home or at a hotel.

The couple must each obtain a marriage notice form from a registrar in any location; when the forms are completed they must be returned to the registrar for the district where the wedding is to take place. This must be done not more than three months and not less than 15 days before the ceremony; the norm is about a month. When the forms are returned you will both have to produce your birth certificates; if either of you has been married before you will also have to show the former spouse's death certificate or a copy of the divorce decree. If either of you is living out of the United Kingdom you will have to declare that there is no legal reason within the regulations of your own country why you cannot be married. If any of the documents are in a foreign language you will need to produce a certified translation.

The registrar will then prepare a marriage schedule. If you are getting married in the registry office they will keep the schedule; if you are getting married in a church or elsewhere one of you must collect the schedule not more than a week before the wedding. After the ceremony the schedule must be signed by both partners, both witnesses, and whoever conducted the wedding; it must be returned to the registrar within three days so that the marriage can be registered.

24

Northern Ireland

In Northern Ireland you must give notice of marriage to the District Registrar of Marriages. The residential qualification is seven days, and marriage can take place by licence, special licence, banns, certificate from a registrar, or licence from a District Registrar of Marriages.

Notices issued in Northern Ireland or Scotland are valid in England and Wales and vice versa, but marriage in a registry office in England or Wales is not possible when one of the partners lives in Northern Ireland or Scotland.

Channel Islands

The Channel Islands are part of the Diocese of Winchester, and the regulations for marriage in church are the same as for the rest of the country.

Marriages abroad

If you are to be married abroad it is vital to find out in advance what documents you will need in order to qualify as legally able to marry. Check carefully any regulations relating to age of the partners, remarriage of divorcees when the partner is still living, proof of residence, proof of no criminal convictions, religious requirements, etc. The exact requirements will vary with the country where the marriage is to take place.

Marriages entered into abroad are generally held to be valid legally in Britain provided that they were valid legally in the country where they took place, and provided that none of the prohibitions of British law (for instance regarding age, kinship, etc) were infringed. British law only recognises monogamous marriages.

Jewish and Quaker weddings

Jewish and Quaker weddings have been outside the jurisdiction of the regulations surrounding the Anglican ceremony since the Marriage Act of 1754; these ceremonies may be conducted in the home if wished, but only Jewish weddings may be conducted out of doors.

Marriage and the law – Controls

Controls and consanguinity

There are still strict controls in England and Wales on who may and may not marry. These are the controls as they stand at present.

- People under 16 years of age may not marry.

- If a person over 16 but under 18 wishes to marry, consent must be obtained from the parents or other lawful guardians or guardian.

- No person who is already married to a living spouse can marry someone else; if they do so the second marriage is invalid.

- No person who is going through a divorce may marry until the decree absolute has been granted.

- The two people wishing to marry must be male and female respectively.

- Both of the people getting married must be acting by their own consent.

- Both of the people getting married must be of sufficiently sound mind to understand the nature of a marriage contract.

An example of a Marriage Certificate

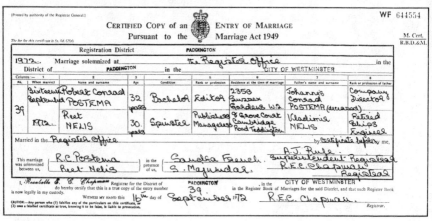

You may not marry your:

mother	daughter's husband
adoptive mother	father's father's wife
former adoptive mother	father's mother's husband
father	mother's father's wife
adoptive or former adoptive father	mother's mother's husband
daughter	wife's father's mother
adoptive or former adoptive daughter	husband's father's father
son	wife's mother's mother
adoptive or former adoptive son	husband's father's father
father's mother	wife's son's daughter
father's father	husband's son's son
mother's mother	wife's daughter's daughter
mother's father	husband's daughter's son
son's daughter	son's son's wife
son's son	son's daughter's husband
daughter's daughter	daughter's son's wife
daughter's son	daughter's daughter's husband
sister	father's sister
brother	father's brother
wife's mother	mother's sister
husband's father	mother's brother
wife's daughter	brother's daughter
husband's son	brother's son
father's wife	sister's daughter
mother's husband	sister's son
son's wife	

Among a tribe in the Philippines, people breaking the taboos of consanguinity were traditionally killed and eaten.

Islam forbids marriage between foster-relations.

Who does what

Who pays for what?

In past times the rules over paying for weddings were very clearly laid out; the bride's father met many of the costs, and the rest were covered by the groom. These days it is much less clear cut. Most couples contribute jointly towards the costs, just as they would towards any other event they were organising together, and often the groom's family also help pay for the wedding or some part of it. Of course the whole issue of who pays for what will be something that you will need to talk about in some detail with both sets of parents, being realistic over what you can all afford. Here, for basic guidelines, are the expenses that are traditionally met by each side, although your own list may look very different!

Bride's family

Press announcements
Invitations
Orders of service
Any other stationery (eg place cards, thank you notes)
Photographs (these may or may not include videos, tape recordings, etc)
The bride's dress and accessories
The bridesmaids' and other attendants' clothes and accessories (although these days many bridesmaids will offer to buy their own)
Flowers for the church
Flowers for the reception
Hen party
Transport for the bride's family to the church, and for the bride's parents to the reception
Hire costs for the reception
Catering costs for the reception
The cake

Groom

Engagement ring
Wedding ring for the bride (the bride traditionally pays for the groom's ring if he has one)
Legal costs (licences, registrar, etc)
Church costs (minister's fee, choir, organist, bellringers, etc)
Flowers for the bride
Flowers for the attendants
Buttonholes for the men in the wedding party
Corsages for the two mothers
Presents for the best man and attendants
Stag party
Transport for himself and the best man to the church, and for himself and the bride to the reception
The honeymoon

Best man

The best man generally pays for his own clothes for the wedding if they have to be made or hired.

Who does what?

Before the wedding there are dozens of details to be worked on and finalised (it will probably seem like thousands at the time!). The details of the wedding used to be the province of the bride's family, with only symbolic consultation with the groom's family, but nowadays couples plan most of the details together. Naturally it is important to consult at every stage with the other participants, such as the bride's parents, the groom's parents, the bridesmaids, the minister, etc, to check that everyone is happy with the wedding plans, but it is a good start to married life if the bride and groom can sort out such major events with plenty of discussion, cross-checking and arrangement-making.

Some of the arrangements will naturally be easier for the bride or for the groom to sort out; others may be easier in consultation with, say, the bride's mother, but here is a list of things that the bride and groom should be sorting out together as the wedding approaches.

- The type of wedding you want – traditional, formal, casual, on a theme, registry office, church
- The date and timing of the wedding and the reception
- Newspaper announcements
- The style of the reception – cocktails, formal meal, buffet, etc
- Who is going to do the catering – professionals, yourselves, family, friends
- The venue of the reception
- The style of service you will have
- Music for the service, reception and evening party if you have one
- Attendants – how many, who, what they will wear
- Flowers for church, reception, bouquets, buttonholes
- Cake – style and size
- Guest list
- Present list
- Wedding stationery – invitations, orders of service, place names, etc
- Photography, video, taping of the service and reception
- Rings – what kind you want, whether you are having one or two
- Transport for everyone to the church and reception
- Presents for attendants
- Stag and bride parties
- Honeymoon

Who does what – Specific responsibilities

Specific responsibilities

In a large, formal wedding, everyone in the wedding party has specific tasks. These tasks will vary according to the details of your wedding, but here are some basic guidelines.

Bride

Buys the groom's ring if he is having one

Holds the bride's party (or hen party) if she is having one

May buy presents for her parents

Plans and selects her own dress and accessories and those of the bridesmaids

Chooses a going-away outfit

Prepares a gift list

Writes thank you notes for gifts received

Makes arrangements for the cake

Her part in the wedding ceremony is to arrive at the church on time, go down the aisle on her father's arm, be married, sign the register, then leave with her husband.

Groom

Plans clothes for himself and the other men

Checks all the legal and practical details of the wedding

His part in the wedding ceremony is to be waiting at the church for the bride, be married, sign the register, then leave with his wife. He will also need to make a speech at the reception.

Bride's mother

Makes out the guest list (in consultation with the groom's family)

Sends out the invitations

Keeps a note of replies

Helps to keep a note of gifts as they arrive, and may make a display of them at her home

May organise the photographs, and take orders afterwards

Helps in arrangements for the cake

Sends out pieces of cake to those who were not able to come to the wedding

The bride's mother traditionally helps the bride to fix the veil (if one is being worn!) before she leaves for the church. She is escorted to her seat, then joins the bridal party for the signing of the register after the marriage. She leaves the church on the arm of the groom's father.

Bride's father

Travels to the church with the bride, then escorts her down the aisle. He gives her away at the appropriate part of the service, witnesses the signing of the register, then leaves the church escorting the groom's mother.

Best man

Arranges the stag night

Instructs the ushers on what to do and when

Checks all the practical arrangements for the day, eg flowers, orders of service, rings, licences, fees

Ensures that the groom has all the documentation that he needs

Checks that all the fees are paid before or after the service

Arranges transport from the service to the reception

Accompanies or drives the groom to the church in good time for the wedding

May act as master of ceremonies at the reception

Gives a speech replying to the toast to the bridesmaids

Reads out any telegrams or important cards (and vets them first for embarrassing references...)

Makes sure that there is a private place for the bride and groom to change

Checks that transport for the honeymoon is in order

Takes charge of the groom's clothes when he has changed

The best man's duties during the ceremony are to be at the front of the church with the groom, to hand over the rings at the appropriate point, to witness the signing of the register, and to escort the chief bridesmaid from the church.

Chief bridesmaid

Helps the bride to dress on the wedding morning

Checks that the bride's going away outfit, etc, travel safely to the reception

Carries emergency supplies for the bride, such as a handkerchief, spare pair of tights, sticking plaster, 'touch-up' make-up

Takes charge of any young attendants during service and reception

Checks that the bride looks her best before she enters the church

Takes charge of the bride's dress after she has changed at the reception

The chief bridesmaid arrives at the church just before the bride, checks that the other attendants know what to do, then goes down the aisle just behind the bride. She takes the bride's bouquet at the front of the church, and may help her to pull back her veil. She witnesses the signing of the register, then leaves the church on the arm of the best man.

Ushers

Show guests arriving at the church where to sit

Hand out orders of service to guests

Ensure that the minister has orders of service at the front for the wedding party

Escort the bride's mother to her seat

Help the best man to ensure that all guests have transport to the reception

Types of ceremony

Choosing a wedding

One of the earliest questions to be settled is the kind of wedding that you want. There are numerous options open to you, and you have the chance to make this most important day live up to all your hopes and expectations for it! Make sure that you choose the type of wedding with which you feel most comfortable. If you have always wanted a large, formal wedding, then go for that option – on the other hand, if you cringe at the thought of all that drama, or if you would be happier with a non-religious ceremony, then don't let anyone push you into a formal church wedding. The basic options for the type of ceremony are set out here; choose the one that fits your own preferences best, and then you can add your own details to it to personalise the day.

Make sure that you discuss things very carefully with the minister or registrar before you start making any definite plans, as there may be certain restrictions on what you can and can't do. For instance, some ministers will not marry divorcees; some ministers may not permit you to marry in church or to wear white if you are living together or are pregnant. Some churches will allow a simple service of blessing after a registry office marriage; some registry offices have restrictions on what can be done in the way of music and flowers. Check beforehand to make sure that you won't be disappointed.

* * *

The formal wedding

Truly formal weddings are awesome affairs, with an equally awesome amount of preparation necessary. The fundamentals of a formal wedding are as follows.

The wedding invitations are engraved or printed to a very high quality, and are worded very formally.

The wedding invitations are sent out by the bride's mother on behalf of the bride's father (or suitable representatives if, for instance, the bride is a stepdaughter or adopted).

The bride wears a formal, floor-length wedding gown of white, cream or ivory, possibly with a train.

The bride wears a veil, which is worn over her face as she goes down the aisle and drawn back before the actual marriage.

The men in the wedding party, and possibly all the guests, wear morning dress; if the male guests don't wear morning dress they will dress in suits.

The female guests wear very formal clothes.

The bride has a maid of honour or chief bridesmaid.

The bride has several other attendants, such as junior bridesmaids, flower girl, pageboys, ringbearer, etc.

The groom has a best man.

The bride is given away by her father or by a close relative or family friend.

The church is decorated by a professional florist.

The bouquets of bride and attendants are professionally made.

You may have pew decorations or ribbon knots inside the church.

Professional musicians play at the service and reception.

The proceedings are recorded by a top-quality photographer, and possibly on video as well.

Formal photographs are taken of the bridal party before the ceremony, the wedding party afterwards, and of all guests.

You must have a wedding cake decorated formally and iced conventionally.

The transport should be very formal such as white or black chauffeur-driven limousines.

The wedding party forms a receiving line as the guests arrive at the reception and greet them individually; there may even be a caller to announce each guest as he or she arrives.

The reception is a formal sit-down meal.

There should be a master of ceremonies to guide the proceedings at the reception, to call upon those who are to make speeches, and to announce the cutting of the cake.

Champagne is provided for the toasts.

Toasts are proposed to the bride and groom and to the bridesmaids.

Any telegrams are read out by the best man.

Confetti is usually thrown over the couple as they leave church or as they leave for honeymoon.

The bride should toss her bouquet among the guests before she goes on honeymoon.

A report of the wedding is sent to the local and/or national papers.

As you can see, a formal wedding is a very serious affair, and any desire for personal touches can be stifled by the requirements of convention. Most couples choose options that allow them somewhat more freedom.

Types of ceremony – Informality

Informal weddings

Informality can be brought into the traditional wedding service in many ways; choose the kind that you feel most comfortable with, and resist any conventions that you feel are inappropriate.

The bride could wear a shorter dress, or one without a train, of less traditional design. She can get married in a suit, in trousers if she wishes, or in a dress that is coloured rather than white.

The bridesmaids can wear less traditional clothes too – for instance tartan or striped cotton rather than pastel satin or net.

The bride may choose not to have any attendants, or may choose a friend who will wear ordinary clothes.

The bouquets could be made up of garden flowers or wild flowers.

The groom and best man may wear ordinary suits or even more casual clothes.

The music could be performed by friends and relations; the couple could even sing themselves, or the music could be taped or from a record if they want something unusual.

The couple may alter the wording of the service itself, or write their own vows.

The minister may wear ordinary clothes rather than vestments.

The couple may introduce non-traditional elements into the service, such as prayers or a blessing from friends, a chance for the congregation to join in well-wishing, a time when they say how they hope to live up to their responsibilities as husband and wife.

The transport may simply be clean, polished cars with ribbons on, or may be less conventional such as an old bus, a vintage car, a horse and carriage.

The reception can be an informal buffet, a cocktail party, or even something as casual as sandwiches or pizza; it can be done by outside caterers or by friends and relations.

The reception may be in an informal setting such as a church hall, a friendly restaurant or a large home.

The speeches can be casual and informal.

The cake can be unusual in design, decoration or recipe.

The music could be personal or unconventional; a specially-written song, a barbershop quartet, even old time music hall!

Registry office weddings

You may choose a registry office wedding because you feel hyprocritical taking religious vows in a church. You may have wanted a church wedding but found it impossible as one of you is divorced, and settled for a registry office ceremony instead. Or you may choose a civil ceremony because you have been living together and don't feel that a church wedding is appropriate, or simply because you want to avoid all the fuss and bother of a church wedding. Whatever your reason, you will find that registry offices are generally attractive places (or at least have an attractive room where the ceremonies take place!). Many registry offices provide flowers in the room and in the lobby, and there may be a garden or ground where pleasant photographs can be taken before and after the wedding. Registry office weddings tend to work out much cheaper than church weddings as so much of the elaborate ceremony is missing, which can be another reason for choosing a civil ceremony!

What you wear is really up to you; you may wish to wear a formal white gown and have attendants and numerous guests, or you may wish simply to wear a beautiful ordinary-length dress and invite only closest friends and relatives. Check with the office itself what arrangements there are for music, taking photographs, whether there is any restriction on the number of guests, etc.

Service of blessing

If you wanted to get married in church but have not been able to because one partner is divorced, it may be possible to have a service of blessing in the church of your choice. Check this with the minister beforehand. You may be able to go to the church from the registry office, or you may choose to have a service of blessing on some other day. The ceremony is usually brief, with prayers, perhaps a hymn, and a blessing; some ministers will not allow the more elaborate details, such as organ music, hymns, bellringing, etc, to take place at a service of blessing.

Types of ceremony – Other religions

Roman Catholic weddings

There have been many changes in the format of Catholic weddings over the last few decades, so there are generally numerous options open to the couple wanting to be married according to the rites of the Catholic church. Since 1836 Catholics (and members of some other religions) have been allowed to marry in their own places of worship, so you should be able to marry in your local Catholic church if you (or your partner) are a regular attender.

The details of the service may vary from one church to another, depending on the tradition favoured by the priest, but there is often quite a lot of flexibility in the ceremony, with the chance for participation from the congregation and from friends taking readings, etc. The ceremonies involved, the nuptial mass, where the wedding party stands or kneels, etc, should all be discussed in detail with the priest as there may be considerable variation between one church and another.

A marriage between a Catholic and someone of another tradition is generally allowed in a Catholic church or a church of another denomination, and often the Catholic priest will be happy to share the duties with another minister of a different religion. Hymns from both traditions may be allowed; this again will depend on the priest's feelings.

At a nuptial mass some of the guests may not be recognised by the Catholic church as communicants (ie those who are allowed to take communion); this problem can be solved by having mass only for the bride and groom or only for the wedding party.

Quaker weddings

From 1754 Quakers have been allowed to abstain from the Anglican ceremony and marry according to their own tradition. Quaker tradition is very plain and the wedding usually reflects this, although the bride may still wear the formal long white gown. It is usual for a couple wanting to be married in a Quaker meeting to apply formally to that meeting by letter; the meeting may then appoint a small group of men and women to talk to the couple and check that they are serious about the ceremony. The Quakers have their own wording for the marriage vows and their own traditions involved in the ceremony.

Jewish weddings

The Marriage Act of 1754 also allowed Jews to carry out their own marriage ceremonies. The precise kind of ceremony will depend on the kind of synagogue that the couple attends – whether it is Orthodox, Conservative or Reformed. Marriage is regarded as the ideal state by the Jewish community, and the ceremony is the legal and spiritual binding of two people and also of two families.

There are many ceremonies that may be involved in a Jewish marriage. One is the Torah honour to the groom; he may be called to read the Torah in the synagogue on the Sabbath before the wedding. In some traditions he is then showered with nuts, raisins and sweets to symbolise the congregation's good wishes for a sweet, fruitful life. Traditionally the bride undergoes the ritual bath just before the wedding day; she should then not see or talk to the groom until the wedding.

In many traditions a Jewish groom will look on his bride while her veil is lifted up and then lower her veil over her face; this is to show publicly that she is the bride he has chosen, and is done in memory of Jacob in the Scriptures, who found himself married to one sister instead of the other because his bride was heavily veiled. The Jewish wedding usually takes place under a canopy (*huppah*), to symbolise the nomadic nature of the Jewish people who for many centuries dwelt in tents. It is customary to have a quorum of at least ten men present at the ceremony.

One of the best-known ceremonies of the Jewish wedding is the breaking of the glass; this is generally done by the groom stamping on it while the guests cry '*Mazal tov!*' The glass-breaking is done to remind the company of the fragility of life in the midst of all the rejoicing. These days the glass is often placed in a bag to avoid sending splinters everywhere.

Other religions

All religions and denominations have their own special words and ceremonies that are customary at weddings. If you are already a member of a particular religious order, you will probably already know which traditions you want to incorporate into your own marriage and reception, but make sure that your minister knows about and approves any significant alterations in the traditional pattern.

Types of ceremony – Alternative options

Alternative weddings

There are many variations on the traditional basic wedding; you may want to have a wedding that is a little bit different because of preference or because of unavoidable circumstances. Here are some of the options for varying your wedding ceremony.

* * *

Military wedding

If one or both of you is in the armed forces, you may wish to have a military style wedding. If the bride is in the forces she will probably prefer a traditional dress to her uniform, while the groom may wear either his dress uniform or his regulation version. If other military personnel are among the guests or attendants they may also wear uniform. The bridal party often leave the church under an arch of crossed swords held by a guard of honour, and a military sword may be used instead of a knife to cut the cake at the reception.

Clergy weddings

If the groom is a minister, the couple may choose to have the wedding at his church rather than at her home church; the groom may wear his vestments or ordinary clothes. It is often customary to invite the entire congregation to attend the wedding service itself, although they don't have to be invited to the reception. If the son or daughter of a minister is marrying the couple may ask that minister to take the ceremony instead of the minister of their chosen church; this generally causes very few problems among the people concerned. Alternatively, the father may be asked to pray for the couple, or to give the address.

Double weddings

Double weddings are most usually conducted when two siblings plan to marry at around the same time; having a double wedding means a saving in time and administration, since many of the same people would be invited to both weddings, and also a considerable saving on cost! The matters of the processions into and out of church, the marriages themselves and the organisation of the speeches, etc, at the reception will need careful planning, but once these details are fixed double weddings can be very special occasions indeed.

Mixed denominations

Marriages can generally be arranged quite easily between people of different denominations; see ministers of the denominations involved and work out how best to conduct the wedding service.

Mixed religions

Some religions will not marry one of their members to a member of another religion; it is important to check this at an early stage. If neither religion will marry you in a religious ceremony, it may be necessary to have a civil ceremony. With certain religions it may be possible to combine the two traditions and have a very personal service designed around their guidelines; this will need to be talked through thoroughly with leaders of both religions to check that it is an acceptable option.

Marriages of older partners

It may be that you and your partner are older than the traditional age for first marriages. In this case, it may well be inappropriate for the wedding to be conducted by the bride's parents as host and hostess, and you may wish to take over all the expenses and the administration yourselves.

Foreign languages

Sometimes one or two of the key people at the wedding, for instance the bride's or groom's parents, do not speak English. In this case it is tactful to have fluent interpreters positioned near them in church and at the reception so that they can take a full part in what is going on. If you are getting married in Wales you may wish to have the ceremony in Welsh; in this case again you should provide an interpreter for those who don't speak the language.

Problems with parents

There is often difficulty if the bride's parents are separated or divorced, or if one of her parents has died. Remember that it is the relationship of the hosts and the bride that is important on the invitations, so these should make it clear if the wedding is being hosted by the bride's mother, stepmother, foster-mother, aunt, etc. If her father is divorced from her mother he may want to contribute to the wedding or to give his daughter away; this depends on her choice, which will probably depend in turn on how close she is to her father, whether she has a stepfather, and whether relations between her natural parents are strained or cordial.

Second weddings

Second weddings

Second weddings are very common with the rising divorce statistics in this country, and are developing an etiquette all of their own.

* * *

Widows and widowers

Of course if you have been married before and your spouse has died, you are quite free to get married in church. Generally a full white wedding with all the trimmings will not be appropriate if the bride has been married before, but may be totally appropriate if it is the groom who is the widower. If the bride is a widow she and the groom will probably share the cost of the wedding, although there is nothing to stop her parents making a contribution.

Where to marry?

Until recently it has been very unusual for Anglican ministers to marry a couple where one of them is divorced and the divorced partner is still living, but there are moves afoot to change this. The Catholic church will only marry a divorced partner if the previous marriage was a civil ceremony (which is not recognised by the church) or if it was annulled. Other denominations tend to act according to the consciences and the preferences of the individual ministers, and their attitudes may vary widely. Remarriage in a synagogue is permitted if both partners have a *Get*, a Jewish religious certificate of divorce; a civil certificate is not enough. Many couples choose to marry in a registry office if one or both is divorced.

Invitations

If it is the bride's first wedding, her family usually contributes towards the cost and hosts the wedding and reception in the usual way. If the bride is divorced, she and her husband-to-be will generally share the costs, but her parents may still offer to pay. If they do host the festivities the invitations can be sent out with the wording: Mr and Mrs Alan Smith request the pleasure of your company at the wedding of their daughter, Alice Higginbottom, to Mr Alexander Jones. If the couple are sending out the invitations themselves they can make them as formal or informal as they wish.

Guests

The divorced partner may have some difficulty over wedding guests; many that he or she wants to invite may have been good friends during their previous marriage. However, if there is any doubt they can always be invited anyway, and they have the freedom to refuse if they feel they cannot attend. It is *not* tactful to invite your former spouse unless you are still on extemely good terms. If you have any children by your previous marriage you should invite them and leave it up to them and your former partner whether they come or not, unless you are having a very small, quiet wedding. If you want them to take an active part in the service, for instance as attendants, ushers, ringbearers, etc, make sure that this is acceptable to your former partner.

What to wear

If the bride is divorced or widowed, it is not really appropriate to go for a full traditional white gown and veil, as these are the symbols of virginity and innocence. However there is nothing to stop you looking pretty and choosing a special dress or outfit in an attractive colour. Some churches may discourage you from having attendants, flowers, bellringing, choirs, etc, if you are remarrying after a divorce; once again it is important to enquire about all these details in good time before you set your heart on a particular kind of ceremony.

Announcements

Some people going through second weddings (or first ones, for that matter!) prefer to keep the ceremony as quiet and private as possible. In this case they may simply invite their very closest friends and relations, or may even choose to get married in front of two independent witnesses such as clerks from the registry office. If the wedding has been quiet, the couple may announce the news in notes – handwritten or printed – to their friends and relations after the event.

Presents

If the bride has been married before she will presumably already have the household things that she needs, but people may still wish to give presents to the couple. If so, it is worth making a friendly enquiry as to what kind of present would be acceptable.

Alternative receptions

Alternative receptions

The wedding service is not the only part of the wedding day that can be varied according to need and preference; the reception also offers the chance for an individual touch.

***

Vegetarian

It is possible to produce delicious vegetarian wedding fare for a formal sit-down meal or for a buffet, but if you want to use a caterer you will probably need to look for one who specialises in vegetarian food.

Kosher

There are numerous tasty traditional Kosher foods that are perfect for weddings, and your families will probably have their own favourites if they are Jewish. Non-Kosher guests are unlikely to find any difficulty over eating Kosher foods.

Teetotal

Teetotal weddings needn't consist of the guests simply drinking orange squash and longing for something more sophisticated! There are many non-alcoholic wines available, both red and white, although they may well be more expensive and certainly harder to obtain than the alcoholic kind. Other alternatives are punches, exotic fruit juices and drinks such as non-alcoholic elderflower champagne.

Low cost

You may be able to afford very little in the way of festivities, but do not despair! If the weather is reliable you could invite everyone to bring a picnic to a pleasant spot in a park, garden or on a riverbank; or you could hire a hall and detail your closest friends and relations to bring a dish each, checking beforehand that you have a good spread of sweet and savoury.

Thematic

You may choose to have your wedding on a particular theme, such as Scottish, Japanese, Victorian; in this case you can choose a reception menu that complements the theme.

Checklist for choosing a wedding

Where do we want to be married?	Do we want lots of guests at the wedding service, or just a few?
Will there be any difficulty if one of us is divorced?	What will the groom wear?
If so, what is our second choice?	
Do we want a formal wedding?	What will the other men attending wear?
Do we want a particular theme?	
Are we trying to cut costs?	What will the minister wear?
Who will give away the bride?	
Does the bride want any bridesmaids?	Who will give the speeches at the reception?
If so, who?	
	Do we want to involve ministers of two denominations or religions?
What about other attendants, such as pageboy, flower girl, ringbearer?	Do we want any interpreters for our guests?
	Do we want any special words or traditions incorporated?
Who will be best man?	
Who will perform the ceremony?	Do we want any alternative kind of reception?

Solving problems

Broken engagement

If the engagement is broken off before the wedding date has been set, let as many people know by word of mouth; you could also put a notice in the paper along the lines of: Mary Jones and David Smith announce that their engagement has been broken by mutual consent.

If the invitations have already been sent out, the bride's parents should send out a message of this kind: Mr and Mrs Harold Jones announce that the marriage of their daughter Mary to Mr David Smith will not now take place. If the wedding presents have been received they should be returned with a polite note from the girl or her mother. The girl may offer to return the engagement ring, and the man may or may not take up the offer. If the wedding dress has already been bought, most shops will take it back and refund the money without any difficulty; if they will not, or if the dress has been specially made, it should be possible to sell it quite easily.

Cancelling the wedding

Occasionally an unprecedented disaster such as a bereavement occurs so close to the wedding that it is impossible to go ahead as planned. In this case the bride's mother should send out a message similar to the following: Owing to the sudden death of Mr Jones, Mrs Jones deeply regrets that the marriage of her daughter Mary to Mr David Smith has been cancelled.

Postponing

If the wedding is to be postponed to a known date, the announcement may read something like this: Because of the illness of the bride's brother, Mr and Mrs Alan Jones have been obliged to postpone the marriage of their daughter Mary to Mr David Smith, which was to have taken place on Saturday, June 14th, to Saturday, August 12th at the same venue.

Cancellation and announcement

If a bereavement has taken place but the couple have decided to go ahead and marry quietly on the planned day or around the same time, the bride's parents may send a message which both cancels the invitations and announces the alternative wedding: Because of the death of the groom's mother, Mr and Mrs Alan Jones regret that they are obliged to cancel the invitations to the wedding of their daughter Mary to Mr David Smith. The wedding was to have taken place on June 14th, but will now take place quietly on June 21st.

Illness

Every bride's dread is that she – or the groom – will be ill on the wedding day. After all the planning, few things are worse than discovering that you are not well enough to enjoy it. If one partner becomes ill some time before the wedding and is obviously not going to be well enough to attend the service, two options are open; you can either postpone the marriage, as above, or you can ask for a special licence from the Archbishop of Canterbury so that the wedding can still take place on the planned day but in the hospital or at the home of the ill partner. In either of these cases.you will need to let your guests know your change of plan.

If one of you is simply too ill on the day itself to go through with the ceremony, for instance as the result of a car accident, you will have no alternative but to cancel or postpone the wedding. It may still be possible to invite the guests to the reception venue so that they at least have a get-together after all their planning and travelling!

If one of the other main participants is ill, such as the best man or the bride's father, it may well be possible to find a last-minute substitute; your guests will understand if things do not run totally smoothly.

Accidents

The other dread of every bride is that something will go wrong; the cake will collapse, the car will get a puncture, she will trip over going up the aisle, or it will pour with rain and soak the whole party. Try to keep a sense of humour and remember that these are the kind of incidents that anecdotes are made of years later. Brides have gone down the aisle with muddy dresses or torn hems, grooms have been married with one foot in plaster or slipped on the chancel steps, but these don't actually matter one jot to the essence of the marriage ceremony itself!

Setting the date and time

Setting the date

Setting the exact date for your wedding may require quite a lot of juggling and manoeuvring. You need to fit it in with your own personal diaries, and also to make sure that all your special guests will be able to join you on the day; you will also need to make sure that all the facilities that you want for the service, the reception and the honeymoon are available.

***

Personal diaries

Your main priority will obviously be to choose a date when neither of you is inextricably booked up for anything else! You will need to look at your work calendars to check that you have no important appointments, and you may need to take your time off during a particular month to fit in with your colleagues at work. This is one good reason for choosing the date of your marriage early, so that you can get in first with your bid for holiday dates. If either of you will be involved with exams, job interviews, long-term projects, etc, you will need to arrange your wedding time around these. Don't forget also that you will need some time clear before the date for the numerous last-minute preparations, and afterwards for the honeymoon and settling into your new home.

Health and weather

If either of you has any health problems these may need to be taken into consideration when setting your wedding date. For instance, if you suffer from hay fever you may wish to avoid your worst months; if you are very prone to colds, bronchitis or flu it will probably be best to avoid an autumn or winter wedding to minimise your chances of being ill on the big day. If you suffer a great deal of discomfort during your periods you may want to plan ahead and try to avoid the worst weeks for your wedding and honeymoon – but remember that weddings are notorious for sending even the most regular menstrual cycle off balance! If lots of your guests will be travelling a long way you will need to take this into account also; it is unfair to inflict long winter journeys on elderly or infirm relatives if they can be avoided.

Family calendars

You will need to make sure that all the people you want to be involved in your wedding will be available on the day that you want. Check your proposed date with both sets of parents, your best man, bridesmaids and other attendants.

Inevitably some of the guests that you invite will be unable to come for one reason or another, but ask around beforehand to ensure that any guests you particularly want to be there will be free on the proposed date.

Finances
It used to be the case that there were certain times of the year that were more advantageous than others for weddings from a tax point of view. This is not currently the case, but watch the budgets to make sure!

Honeymoon
You may need to set the date of your wedding during a particular month because of your choice of honeymoon. For instance, if you want to have a walking holiday in the Lake District you would do best to avoid a wedding in the depths of winter; if you want to catch the sun in Australia, it is no use getting married in midsummer here!

Availability
Once you have sorted out your personal diaries, one of the main considerations will be the availability of the venues that you want to use. Many churches get booked up for weddings many months in advance, so talk to the minister early on in your plans so that you won't be disappointed. Church weddings used not to be allowed during the main church festivals, such as Lent and Advent, but this is no longer the case. Check also that there will be someone available to marry you – remember that ministers have holidays and unavoidable engagements just like the rest of us! Check also on the venue that you want for your reception; once again, picturesque or well-known restaurants and hotels may be booked up months in advance.

Setting the date – Traditions

Traditions

There are numerous traditions about the best time to marry; the most common time in this country is in the summer, generally because it fits well into people's work and holiday schedules, but if it suits you and yours best there is no reason why you shouldn't be married at any time of the year you choose. Weddings are generally not allowed in churches on Sundays and in synagogues on the Jewish sabbath (sundown Friday to sundown Saturday), but other days are generally acceptable. Most people choose to get married on a Saturday as this ensures that the maximum number of guests will be able to get time off work to attend, but if you are having a quiet wedding, particularly at a registry office, you don't need to be tied to a Saturday.

Here are some traditional rhymes relating to the month and day of weddings.

Marry when the year is new,
Always loving, kind and true.
When February birds do mate
You may wed or dread your fate.
If you wed when March winds blow
Joy and sorrow both you'll know.
Marry in April when you can –
Joy for maiden and for man.
Marry in the month of May
You will surely rue the day.
Marry when June roses blow,
Over land and sea you'll go.
They who in July do wed,
Must labour always for their bread.
Whoever wed in August be
Many a change are sure to see.
Marry in September's shine,
Your living will be rich and fine.
If in October you do marry
Love will come, but riches tarry.
If you wed in bleak November,
Only joy will come, remember.
When December snows fall fast,
Marry and true love will last.

Monday for health,
Tuesday for wealth,
Wednesday the best day of all;
Thursday for losses,
Friday for crosses,
Saturday no luck at all.

Married in January's frost and rime,
Widowed you'll be before your time.
Married in February's sleety weather,
Life you'll tread in tune together.
Married when March winds shrill and roar,
Your home will be on a foreign shore.
Married 'neath April's changeful skies,
A chequered path before you lies.
Married when bees or May-blooms flit,
Strangers around your board will sit.
Married in queen-rose month of June,
Life will be one long honeymoon.
Married in July's flower-banks' blaze,
Bitter-sweet memories in after days.
Married in August's heat and drowse,
Lover and friend in your chosen spouse.
Married in gold September's flow,
Smooth and serene your life will flow.
Married when leaves in October thin,
Toil and hardship for you begin.
Married in veils of November mist,
Fortune your wedding ring has kissed.
When December's snows fall fast,
Marry and true love will last.

Setting the date – Checklist/Timetable

Checklist for date

What time of year do we want to be married – spring, summer, autumn or winter?	Are the people we want to take part available on the date we are thinking of? Best Man
Where do we want to spend our honeymoon? Will this make any particular demands on the date for our wedding?	Bridesmaids Bride's parents Groom's parents
Are there any dates that we cannot be married or go on honeymoon, because of immovable commitments? Bride Groom	Is the church or registry office available on that day?
	Is the minister or registrar available?
	Is the reception venue available on that day?

Checklist for time

Do we want a morning or afternoon wedding?	How long will it take to get everyone from the service to the reception?
Do we want a meal at the reception, or just snacks?	
	What time do we want to get away on honeymoon?
If we want a full meal, will it be lunch or tea or dinner?	What time will the wedding be?
	What time will the reception start?

Times

Once you know the date that you want, and are sure that all the facilities you want are available, you will need to decide on the timing of the service and reception.

Service

First of all, check whether there are any other weddings booked at the church or registry office on your chosen day. If there are, this may restrict your choice of times. If you have the whole day to choose from you will need to decide whether you want to be married in the morning or the evening. All weddings take place between 8 am and 6 pm – the only exceptions to this are Jewish and Quaker ceremonies and weddings performed under special licences or licences from the Registrar General. This restriction was brought in to minimise the chances of illicit weddings by ensuring that the wedding was in daylight (more or less!) so that everyone could see the participants.

Working out the timetable

The wedding service itself is not very long; with hymns, the signing of the register and the processional music it will probably still take well under an hour. However, you will need to allow time outside the church or registry office for photographs and chatting, and it will take quite a time to make sure that everyone has transport to the reception and that there are no stragglers. Then you will have to consider the time it takes to get from the church to the reception – how long is the journey? What will the traffic be like? Once at the reception you will have to build in time for the guests to leave their coats, go to the toilet, be met and chatted to by the receiving line, be provided with a drink, etc. Once everyone has arrived you can go ahead with the meal, buffet or snacks; allow a sensible amount of time for the food before the speeches, toasts and cake-cutting. You may want to slip away at this stage and change for the honeymoon, or you may want to stay and chat for a bit. When fixing your timetable definitely, begin with the most important and crucial time. This may be that you have to be at the airport for the 6.30 plane, or it may be that the hotel serves lunch at 12.30; work your own timetable out from these immutables, remembering that most stages will need more time than you think rather than less!

Guests

Choosing your guests

Choosing the wedding guests can be one of the most contentious parts of the wedding preparations, as the different people involved may have different priorities. Parents and parents-in-law will often want to invite relations of all degrees as the wedding is a rare chance for a full-scale family get-together. Bride and groom are often more interested in inviting friends that are more immediate – colleagues from work, close friends from school and college days, etc. So you will all need great tact and consideration to avoid falling out over this most crucial question.

Relations

Happy the bride and groom with few relations! This makes for a guest list that is simple to put together. However, if you have numerous relations scattered all over the country (or even nearby), you will have to make the difficult choice of which ones to invite and which ones to leave out. Are they close family friends as well as relations? Have they always taken an interest in the bride or groom, or have they rarely seen them? Will they expect to be invited? Will they be offended if they aren't invited? Are you going to set a limit of consanguinity – for instance invite anyone up to a first cousin, and no-one beyond that?

Friends

These fall into two categories – friends of the family, and friends of the bride and groom. They can be anything from the girl next door or childhood playmate to college room-mate or best friends at the club. The bride and groom may have to be ruthless about which of these friends can and cannot be invited. If both bride and groom are from the town where the wedding is taking place, it may be possible to invite work colleagues, casual friends, etc, to come and see the marriage service even though there might not be room for them at the reception. Obviously this doesn't work so well if the wedding is some distance away from the groom's home town. Some couples surmount the problem by having an informal party in the evening for friends, so that they don't feel they've missed out.

Practicalities

The invitations are generally sent out by the bride's mother or the bride herself, so the groom's mother usually supplies a list of relations and friends who should be invited from their side. Although it is the bride's family that pays for the reception, it is a little unfair for her to have substantially more guests than the groom; the best idea is to set a rough number of guests as a total and to suggest that the groom's family supplies half that number.

The number of guests you can invite will probably be limited by two factors: the capacity of the place where you will be having the reception (or, occasionally, the capacity of the church), and the amount of money you have earmarked for the reception. Of course, if you realise that you have budgeted for 60 guests and you would really like 75, it is perfectly possible to economise a little in some other area, for instance by offering a simpler menu or by cutting out one of the hired wedding cars – it all depends on your priorities.

Special requirements

Guests who live in distant parts of the country – or perhaps even abroad – will probably need overnight accommodation for one or more nights. Ask around tactfully among your friends and relations near the town where the wedding is to be; the bride's parents may be able to put up some of the guests, but remember that they will have plenty to do at the last minute without having to be host and hostess as well. An alternative is to book the guests into a bed and breakfast guest-house, either at your expense or at theirs.

Guests from far afield will find it invaluable to have a map and written instructions for finding the church or registry office and the location of the reception. Guests from the locality may still need instructions for getting from one to the other. Transport may also be a problem: make a list beforehand of who will go in whose car, so that no-one is left without a lift on the day.

Children can be invited with their parents, or you can invite the parents only at your discretion. Make it clear one way or the other on the invitations. If children are being invited make sure that the reception is suitable for them – for instance, is there somewhere where they can play if they get bored?

Suggest to your guests that they indicate any special requirements when they accept the invitation – for instance, special diets, need of transport, use of a high chair at the reception, wheelchair bound, etc. Then you will be able to make sure that your guests enjoy your wedding day as much as you do.

Guests – Invitation checklist

Guest list

Use this list to record the people you have invited to your wedding, their answer, the number of children they will be bringing, and any special requirements they have.

Name of guest	Accepted	Refused	Children	Special needs

Name of guest	Accepted	Refused	Children	Special needs

Invitations

Invitations

Your invitations are the first part of your official wedding stationery; they serve both a practical and a decorative purpose. It is worth putting quite a lot of thought into your invitations and how they relate to any other stationery you will be using; the invitations should be a pleasure to send as well as to receive.

***

The information

Your invitations will need to make it clear who is hosting the celebrations, who is getting married, where it will take place (church or registry office and town), the exact date and time, precisely who is invited, whether an RSVP is required, and to whom the reply should be addressed. Many invitations will also include details of the reception. It is not generally necessary to include the year in the date. If you are happy to receive RSVPs by phone then just put a telephone number instead of an address; a phone number can often be useful anyway in case the guest has to cancel or alter arrangements at the last minute.

Making them special

There are many ways in which you can make your wedding invitations personal and unique. Most large stationers' have formula wedding stationery where your names and details are just slipped into a pre-set style, but you may well want to do something more special. You may want to go to a small printer rather than a chain store so that you can get a personal service. You will then have more freedom to choose the colour of the card and ink, to include motifs, borders, monograms, pictures, special typefaces, etc. Some firms will draw a picture of your church, write each invitation out calligraphically, or even embroider your invitations.

How many?

Remember that each couple, and each family with children, needs only one invitation. If the children are over 18 they should be sent their own invitation, even if they live at home. Print some extras though for albums, to allow for mistakes, and in case there are last minute additions to the guest list.

Other stationery

While you are enquiring about invitations, take the opportunity to decide what other matching stationery you will require, such as orders of service, books of matches, thank you notes, etc.

Styles of invitation

Choose your invitations to fit in with the style of your wedding as a whole. The design and layout can be formal, informal, traditional, modern, hand-written, etc; the invitations can include a photograph, a monogram, a drawing of the couple or of relevant symbols (for instance, notes if you are musicians, a hospital crest if you are doctors, etc), attractive borders, and any number of other touches to make your invitations stand out from the crowd.

Three styles of invitation
1 Traditional, formal
2 Modern, formal
3 Modern, informal

1

Mr and Mrs James Evans
request the pleasure of
your company at the marriage
of their daughter
Anna
to
Mr Alan Montague
at St. Mary's Church, Staveley,
on Saturday, 8th September, 1990
at 3 o'clock
and afterwards at
The White Swan, Staveley.

R.S.V.P
138 Ro... Road,
Stave...
Y...

2

John and Eilish
invite

to
the blessing of their marriage
at
Holy Trinity Church
Hurstpierpoint
Sussex
on
Saturday 25th August 1990
at 3·30 pm
and afterwards at
The Bolney Stage
London Road
Bolney
R.S.V.P
20 Kemps, Hurstpierpoint, Sussex

3

Richard & Jane
invite

to their marriage at
Christchurch, Sevenoaks,
Kent
on Saturday, 20th October 1990
at 3 o'Clock
and afterwards at
the "Pied Bull", Sevenoaks,

*

R.S.V.P to
16 Mayfield Avenue
Sevenoaks
Kent

*

Invitations – Wording/Variations

Wording

There are rules for the wording of very formal invitations, but do remember that these can always be varied if the wedding is anything other than the most formal high society affair. The most important point to clarify on the invitations is the relationship between the bride and whoever is hosting the celebrations.

If the bride's parents are hosts:
Mr and Mrs Alan Brown request the pleasure of your company at the wedding of their daughter Ann to John Smith...

If the bride's parents are divorced, but hosting the wedding together:
Mr Alan Brown and Mrs Jane Brown... of their daughter Ann...

If the bride is marrying for the second time but the parents are still the hosts:
Mr and Mrs Alan Brown... of their daughter Ann Jones...

If the mother is widowed and is the sole host:
Mrs Alan Brown... of her daughter Ann...

If the mother is divorced and not remarried:
Mrs Jane Brown... of her daughter Ann...

If the mother is divorced or widowed and remarried:
Mrs Jane Fletcher... of her daughter Ann Brown....

If the mother has remarried and she and the stepfather are joint hosts:
Mr and Mrs Robert Fletcher... of her daughter Ann Brown...

If the mother has remarried but she and the bride's father are joint hosts:
Mrs Robert Fletcher and Mr Alan Brown (or Mr Alan Brown and Mrs Robert Fletcher)... of their daughter Ann Brown...

If the bride's father is sole host:
Mr Alan Brown... of his daughter Ann...

If the bride's stepfather is sole host:
Mr Robert Fletcher... of his stepdaughter Ann Brown...

If the bride's foster-parents are hosts:
Mr and Mrs Andrew Lawrence... of their foster-daughter Ann Brown...

If the bride's godmother is host:
Mrs Peter Mitchell...of her goddaughter Ann Brown...

If the bride's godmother and her husband are hosts:
Mr and Mrs Peter Mitchell...of her goddaughter Ann Brown...

If the bride's uncle and aunt are hosts:
Mr and Mrs Christopher Roberts...of their niece Ann Brown...

If a friend is host:
Miss Jennifer Williams...of Ann Brown...
or:
Mr Johnathan Potter...of Ann Brown...

There are, of course, numerous variations even on these possibilities!

Double weddings

If two daughters of the same couple are getting married the elder one is mentioned first on the invitation. If the same couple are acting as hosts for the wedding of a daughter and a niece or goddaughter, the daughter is mentioned first. If two couples are acting as joint hosts for a double wedding, the older couple is mentioned first.

Variations

Some couples decide to have an evening party for a wider group of friends and relatives; in this case you may wish to have special invitations printed with just the evening details. Registry offices are often quite small and it may not be possible to invite everyone to the service; in this case you can send an invitation just to the reception, including a note of explanation if you wish. It used not to be correct to invite people to the service only, but this is no longer the case; friends from work, church, sports clubs, etc, will often appreciate the chance to witness the service. If there are only a few in this category you could invite them by word of mouth; if there are more than a few you could have invitations printed, just giving details of the service and omitting the reception details.

Invitations – Procedure/Checklist

Sending out the invitations

The invitations should be sent out by the bride's family (generally by her mother) if the bride's parents are hosting the wedding. If the bride and groom are doing it themselves, the bride should send them out. By convention the invitation is addressed to the wife if it is sent to a couple; the wife replies, addressing her reply to the bride's mother. On the invitation the couple can either be addressed formally as Mr and Mrs Robert King, less formally as Robert and Anita King, or informally as Robert and Anita, depending on how formal the wedding is and how well the hosts know the people being invited. Always make it clear on an invitation whether children are invited; this saves embarrassment later. If you are inviting a whole family, the invitation can read Mr and Mrs Robert King and family; Robert and Anita King, Harriet, Emily and James; or Robert, Anita, Harriet, Emily and James.

Inclusions

If there is any possibility that the guests will not know exactly how to get to the church or reception, include a photocopied sketch map with the invitations, marking all the relevant points. You may also wish to include a gift list with the invitations (see the section on presents), although this does tend to look a little grasping! Even if you are going to send a gift list out to all the guests, it is more tactful to do so at a later stage.

Acceptances

Generally, formal invitations require formal acceptances, written in the third person; for instance Mr and Mrs Geoffrey Waters thank Mr and Mrs Brown for their kind invitation and will be delighted... or regret they cannot... However, more and more people these days reply to invitations informally, and are more likely to write something such as Geoff and Margaret Waters will be delighted... or we will be delighted... signed, Geoff and Margaret. Keep a log of replies (see pp 54–55) and also a running total; don't forget to tell the caterers, etc, if the total is very different from the numbers originally expected.

In Bulgaria, wedding invitations traditionally took the form of cakes sent out by the bride's parents.

*

In ancient rural Germany, a person known as a 'wedding inviter' was employed to do the job; the man was decorated with flowers and ribbons and carried a decorated stick to knock on the guests' doors.

Checklist for invitations

How many invitations will we need?
What style of invitations do we want?
Do our stationer's have anything suitable, or do we want them designed and printed specially?
What colour paper do we want?
What colour ink?
Do we want a monogram?
Do we want a photograph or picture?
Are there any other personal touches we want incorporated?
What wording do we want?
Who will be printing the invitations?
How much will they cost?
How far in advance will we have to order them?
When will we have to collect them?

Wedding presents

Presents

Traditionally presents are given to the couple getting married to help them set up their own home together. Consequently wedding presents are often practical household items – this is the tradition in many countries throughout the world.

* * *

Gift lists

It is often sensible to compile a list of the items that you are in need of in your new home, or that would make appropriate wedding presents. If you want an item that is a specific brand or colour it is important to make this clear so that everyone knows where they stand. Remember to include items at many different price levels so that there is something that everyone can afford. There are various ways of distributing the gift list before a wedding. One is to photocopy a list such as the one overleaf and distribute it to all the guests, asking them to cross off the item that they will be buying and return it to the bride. Another way is to send round just one master list for people to choose from; they can cross off the chosen item and then return the list to the bride or send it on to the next person on the guest list, which could be attached. A third way is to choose a shop within easy reach of most of the guests and compile a list there; the shop will then hold the list for you, and anyone wishing to buy a present can enquire there and choose from the items the couple have selected. A fourth way is for the bride to hold the list and wait for people to enquire; she can then suggest two or three possible options, suiting them to the guest's circumstances and pocket.

At high-class Japanese weddings the gifts can include substantial pieces of furniture such as beds, tables, screens and chests. These and the smaller gifts used to be carried through the streets by long lines of bearers.

Money

Some guests may prefer to give money as a wedding present. They may leave it up to a couple to choose how they use it, or they may suggest that it is towards a car or for a cooker, for instance. Even if the use is not specified, it is a nice gesture when writing to say thank you to tell the giver how you intend to use the money.

'If it were not for the presents, an elopement would be preferable'. Ade

Alternative presents

Household items are not the only kind of wedding presents that are acceptable. Often when the couple has already acquired a good deal of household equipment they will not need much in this line; then they may suggest to guests they give presents that are decorative or beautiful, such as prints, vases, ornaments, etc. There is nothing wrong in suggesting unusual wedding gifts to guests, such as plants for the garden, utensils and recipe books for gourmet cooking, books on a favourite subject. If a guest has a particular talent you might suggest that they make or do something for you instead, such as service your car, make your wedding dress, carve you a name plaque, sing at your wedding, plant your vegetable patch. Many people would prefer to feel that they have been able to give something that is a little more personal than a shop-bought gift.

In the traditions of the Mezökövesd district of Hungary all the household presents are piled onto an open wagon; the pile can be enormous and very precarious! The bride and groom then drive off to their new home.

Keeping check

It can be a bit of a nightmare keeping tabs on just who has given what present, especially if many of the presents only arrive on the day and may have separated from their gift labels by the time you return from honeymoon! Start a log-book as soon as the first present arrives and list the gift and the giver; leave a column at the end to tick when a thank you has been sent. It is proper to thank everyone in writing, even though it can seem a chore at the time. Do all the thank you notes you can before the day itself, then the remaining ones will not seem such a daunting task. Some couples have special thank you notes printed; these can be very attractive, but do try and add a personal note to each one to show that the present really has been appreciated.

In Venice, brides used to be expected to provide all of the furniture for the new house; if this was impossible she had to provide at least the bedroom furniture – a bed of walnut wood, six chairs, two chests of drawers, and a looking glass.

Wedding presents – Gift lists

Gift lists

These lists provide ideas for the basic household items that may be useful to you as wedding presents; you could use this as a starting point for your own list, or photocopy this list and circulate it among your guests. Obviously each couple will be different in what they require and what they already have; add your own individual wants or needs such as a yogurt-maker, sandwich toaster, pictures, fire irons, paints and brushes, etc!

Household items

Item	Make/style	Colour
Barbecue		
Bath mat		
Bath rack		
Bedspread		
Blankets		
Candlesticks		
Clock		
Dustpan and brush		
Duvet		
Duvet cover		
Electric blanket		
Iron		
Ironing board		
Lamps		
Linen basket		
Pedal bin		
Pillowcases		
Pillows		
Salt and pepper set		
Sheets		
Tablecloths		
Table mats		
Teatowels		
Toast rack		
Tools		
Towels		
Trays		
Vases		
Waste paper baskets		

Kitchen items

Item	Make/style	Colour
Baking tins and trays		
Bread bin		
Bread board and knife		
Casseroles		
Cheeseboard and knife		
Coffee percolator		
Colander		
Corkscrew		
Deep fryer		
Dish drainer		
Doormat		
Egg whisk		
Flan dishes		
Flask		
Food processor		
Food scales		
Frying pans		
Kettle		
Kitchen tools		
Knife rack		
Knife sharpener		
Mixing bowls		
Potato peeler		
Ramekins		
Rolling pin		
Salad bowl		
Saucepans		
Sieve		
Slow cooker		
Spice rack		
Storage jars		
Tea strainer		
Toaster		
Vegetable rack		
Wooden spoons		
Wok		

Wedding presents – Gift lists

Crockery

Item	Number	Make/style	Colour
Plates – small			
– large			
– medium			
Soup bowls			
Vegetable dishes			
Cereal/dessert bowls			
Other serving dishes			
Sugar bowl			
Milk jug			
Cream jug			
Coffee cups and saucers			
Teacups and saucers			
Butter dish			
Mugs			
Egg cups			
Other crockery			

Glassware

Item	Number	Make/style
Decanters		
Jampot		
Fruitbowl		
Other glassware		

Cutlery

Item	Number	Make/style
Knives		
Forks		
Dessert spoons		
Dessert forks		
Soup spoons		
Fish knives		
Fish forks		
Teaspoons		
Coffee spoons		
Serving spoons		
Butter knives		
Steak knives		
Salad servers		
Ladle		
Carving knife		
Others		

Other presents

Item	Number	Make/style	Colour

Wedding presents – Gift record

Gift record

Use this chart to record gifts as you receive them, the name of the sender, and when you have sent them a thank you note.

Present	Sender	Thank you

Present	Sender	Thank you

Wedding presents – Gift record/Thank you notes

Gift record

Present	Sender	Thank you

Thank you notes

To make your task easier, many firms now print special thank you notes.
These can be printed specially with your names to match your wedding
stationery, or you can buy packs of thank you cards from ordinary stationers'
shops and add your own message.

Budgeting

How much will it cost?

Getting married is notoriously expensive. Some couples are more than happy to spend out a great deal on this, the most showy day of their lives; others may have to save money wherever they can, especially if the bride and groom are footing all the bills themselves. Although the bride's father traditionally pays for the largest part of the wedding, these days many couples contribute to the costs. Whoever is paying, it is worth finding out beforehand just how much each stage of the wedding is likely to cost so that you can budget accordingly and cut costs if necessary. That way all of you will be saved nasty surprises when the bills arrive!

* * *

Clothes

The clothes that are bought or made ready for the big day can eat up a sizable part of your budget. The wedding dress is often the focus of the preparations for the bride, and not surprisingly; she wants to look her very best on this special occasion, and having the dress of her dreams may be part of that. Many wedding dresses can be bought for around £200 or less, but the material is unlikely to be of first-class quality; for anything a bit special you are more likely to pay about £400 or more. Of course some incredible creations can leave you little change out of £1,000, but few brides (or their fathers!) can spare that much for one garment. Costs can be reduced considerably by making your own dress or having it made, and you will certainly be able to afford something more special for the price you would have paid for an off-the-peg dress. Hiring or borrowing is, or course, even cheaper.

If you have a limited budget for your dress, don't let sales staff pressurise you into buying something beyond it; this is another good reason for having someone with you for moral support. Insist that they show you dresses that are within or very near your price range. And don't forget the cost of all the accessories, these can add up alarmingly quickly. Bridal shops can charge you a lot for accessories such as shoes, headdresses, underskirts, hats, etc; if possible get them somewhere else, where they will be much better value, or in the case of things like headdresses and petticoats you could make your own.

Many grooms have a new suit made for the wedding, and generally this will cost at least £100 if it is made-to-measure; an off-the-peg one will be cheaper if you can find a good fit. Hiring morning suits or other clothes is not terribly expensive, but it does mean that the best man and the other men in the wedding party, such as the bride's father, groom's father and ushers, will also have to pay to hire similar outfits.

Clothes for the attendants, especially if you have lots of bridesmaids and pageboys, can also be very expensive. Many bridesmaids these days contribute at least something towards the cost of their outfits but you should not demand that they do so. As with the bride's outfit there are many 'hidden' expenses such as the bridesmaids' shoes, headdresses, petticoats, etc.

Rings
Engagement rings are often bought before the couple start to count the cost of the wedding, so you may have been more extravagant at this stage than you will be later! The cost of an average engagement ring is around £200, but of course they can be much cheaper or very much more expensive. Wedding rings tend to be cheaper as they are not generally set with stones or of unusual designs; the cost will probably be under £100 each unless they are of platinum or very heavy rings in 18ct gold. Some couples just buy a wedding ring for the bride, but more and more grooms these days are wearing rings too, and this of course doubles the expense.

Stationery
If you have your wedding stationery specially printed with your own details you can expect to pay around £80–£100 for invitations and orders of service; the price will vary depending on how many of each you order. If you have your stationery designed for you the cost could be more or less, depending on the intricacy of the design and whether you want any special card, etc. If you extend the range of your stationery with matchbooks, placecards, tablecloths, serviettes, thank you notes, etc, your bill will be still higher.

Budgeting – How much will it cost?

Transport

Many a bride dreams of arriving at the church in a white Rolls Royce – but you may start to have nightmares when you look into prices! If you are hiring all the main cars for a wedding then you will need at least two and probably three or four; each can cost well over £100. And, if course, if you want anything more fancy such as a vintage car or a horse and carriage the costs will be still steeper. Ask for estimates from as many firms as you can so that you can be sure you are getting the best deal.

Photography

Unless you have a very skilled photographer among your relatives or wedding guests, it is best to entrust the photography on the big day to a professional. Firms vary widely in what they offer; some have a flat fee for the day and a certain number of prints; others will charge for the orders taken. The average price is around £200 for a fairly standard service; some firms offer a variety of special effects, or special ways of mounting or presenting the photographs, but these extras can be very expensive. Many couples these days choose to take advantage of modern technology and have their services and receptions recorded on video; naturally this will add to the expense.

Flowers

Considering the attractive part they play in any wedding, professionally arranged flowers are not prohibitively expensive. Bouquets may be around £15 each for a simple style, somewhat more for more extravagant designs or if you have requested specific flowers that may be hard to obtain. Flower arrangements for the church and reception can be arranged similarly; check how much the florist is likely to charge for these and decide how many you want according to your budget. Many couples have corsages made up for the mothers of the bride and groom; these are not terribly expensive. Buttonholes for the men in the wedding party are a nice finishing touch; if you are feeling very generous or are working to a large budget, you may choose to provide buttonholes for all the guests.

Reception

The reception is often the largest figure in the budget. As well as the cost of hiring the hall, hotel or restaurant there is often a full meal provided for a considerable number of guests. On top of this comes the drinks bill, which can be very large when sherry, wine, champagne for the toasts and after-dinner port are included. If you are having a formal reception for, say, 75 guests you will probably spend the best part of £1000 by the time you have also paid for the cake to be made and iced.

Evening party
Many couples fund an evening party for their friends out of their own pockets; with hall hire, drinks, music and food this can easily cost £200 or more, even if there is no full meal laid on. Of course you could save on this sum or be more extravagant if you choose.

Honeymoon
Lots of couples go abroad for their honeymoon, not least so that they can try and ensure that they have constant sunshine! Even the cheapest package holiday for a fortnight will probably cost several hundred pounds with spending money and meals, and anything more luxurious will be accompanied by an appropriate increase in the bill.

Pre-wedding routines
If you want to look your best on the big day, you may well choose to have a facial, manicure, sauna, etc, beforehand. Some brides also choose to be made up professionally as a once-in-a-lifetime treat. And don't forget the cost of having your hair done for the day.

Official fees
There will inevitably be official fees for your wedding licence, minister's fees, registrar, etc; check beforehand exactly what these will be. If you are getting married in church you may have to pay the organist and almost certainly the choir and bellringers if you want their services; the minister will advise you on the appropriate fees.

Budgeting – Cutting the cost

Cutting the cost

You may be beginning to despair and thinking 'How can we ever afford to get married if that's what it's going to cost?' But all is not lost; there are numerous ways of cutting down on the costs incurred by a traditional wedding. Even if you have a more or less unlimited budget it is silly to pay out unnecessarily for details that you are not that bothered about, so you might find some of these ideas useful. If you are on a very limited budget these ideas could make all the difference between a disappointing wedding day and one that is full of most of the traditional trimmings – but at less than the traditional cost!

In rural England bride-ales were common. A small party would be held in the church after the ceremony, then a collection box would be sent round. Alternatively, guests could throw money into a bowl in the church before or after the service.

Clothes

Make your own wedding and bridesmaids' dresses, or have them made for you by a friend or relation.
Cut down on your anticipated number of bridesmaids, pageboys, etc.
Hire your wedding dress, groom's suit, etc.
Use a suit that the groom has already rather than getting one made.
Borrow or hire a veil.
Wear a pair of white shoes you already have rather than buying new ones.
Use your best dress as your going-away outfit.

In some areas of rural France there used to be a traditional way of raising money for couples who could not afford the whole cost of getting married. The five prettiest girls in the village were sent from house to house; the first offered food, the second offered wine, the third received the money, the fourth wiped the donor's mouth with a napkin, and the fifth gave him a kiss.

Flowers

Make your own bouquets, or ask a friend to do it for you.
Carry posies of flowers from your garden.
Cut down on the number of arrangements in the church and at the reception.

Reception

Cut down the number of guests anticipated.

Use a church hall instead of an hotel or restaurant.

Do the catering yourself, or ask friends to help.

Ask your guests to bring some food.

Have snacks or cocktails rather than a full meal.

Have a pay-your-own-way bar.

Use cheaper wine rather than champagne for the toasts.

Make and ice your own cake, or ask a friend.

Honeymoon

Borrow a cottage or a villa.

Go somewhere in this country rather than abroad.

Go on a special budget deal holiday.

Take your honeymoon at off-peak season.

Go to a bed and breakfast or self-catering place.

Stay at home!

In Finland, brides traditionally sat in splendour with a rich shawl over their knees at the wedding feast; as each guest filed past he or she would place some money in the shawl.

Extras

Marry in a registry office and save on the church trimmings.

Use smart cars belonging to friends and relations, and trim them with white ribbon, rather than hiring.

Ask a friend with a video camera to record the proceedings for you instead of a professional company.

Cut down on the number of pictures you have taken.

Hand-write all your invitations.

Have one ring instead of two.

Buy rings made of 9ct gold or silver instead of 18ct gold or platinum.

Cut down on extra stationery such as place cards, thank you notes, etc.

*

Some wedding firms offer a special budgeting service; it may be worth looking into one of these if money is likely to be a problem.

Budgeting – Checklist

Planning your budget

Use this list to plan your own wedding budget. Fill in your own maximum sums in the space provided and also fill in who will be responsible for that particular cost.

	£	Who will pay?
Bride's dress		
Veil		
Shoes		
Headdress		
Hairstyle		
Beauty treatments		
Bridesmaids' dresses		
Accessories for bridesmaids		
Groom's clothes		
Groom's accessories		
Pageboy's clothes		
Ushers' clothes		
Bouquets		
Buttonholes		
Corsages		
Bouquets for mothers		
Flowers at the church		
Flowers at the reception		
Transport		
Minister's fee		
Licence		
Choir		
Bellringers		
Organist		
Soloists		
Other musicians		

Wedding stationery		
Making the cake		
Icing the cake		
Rings		
Photographs,		
Video		
Tape recording		
Wedding album		
Hire of reception venue		
Caterers or food		
Drink with the meal		
Champagne		
Hire of evening party venue		
Food for evening party		
Drink for evening party		
Gifts for attendants		
Presents for parents		
Presents for each other		
Transport to honeymoon		
Going-away outfits		
Honeymoon travel		
Honeymoon accommodation		
Spending money		
Clothes for honeymoon		
New luggage		
Change of address cards		
Fee for changing passport		

What is the total cost?
Is it fairly allocated among bride and groom, bride's parents, groom's parents?
Is there anywhere that we need to cut down?
If so, where?

Pre-wedding parties

Pre-wedding parties

Marriage is the beginning of a whole new life together, and there are many traditions of the bride and groom holding parties separately with their own friends of the same sex while they are still single – usually soon before the wedding. You may not like the idea of having a 'final fling' while you are still supposedly unfettered, but there is nothing to stop you enjoying a unique get-together with your own particular friends before your wedding day.

* * *

Stag parties

Stag parties – so called because only males are invited – are often in the news because of the atrocities perpetrated on the groom-to-be in the way of practical jokes. These are often in dubious taste, and can traditionally take the form of getting him drunk – so, even if you think you know your friends, beware! The best man is supposed to organise the stag night; if he doesn't know all of your close friends you may need to give him a list of whom to invite. Never, never let him arrange a stag night for the evening before the wedding; you may suffer nothing worse than a hangover, but grooms have been known to wake up on their wedding morning on a cross-channel ferry or a train to Aberdeen! Insist that the stag night is held earlier, preferably about a week before the wedding to let you get over any ill effects.

The stag night that is nothing more than a booze-up is crashingly boring; why not think up something more original (or allow your best man to!) You could have a tennis party, a trip to the theatre, a card-playing evening, or even a fancy dress party. Or you could simply all go out for a good meal.

In Morocco the groom has what is traditionally called 'the cleaning of the wheat' or 'the bridegroom's day of cleaning.' Four flags are hoisted over the house, then bags of grain that are to be used for the wedding feast are heaped up in the courtyard. The grain is then cleaned by unmarried girls of the family or from the neighbourhood.

Bride's parties

Bridal parties are more traditional in America than they are in this country. In America the bride usually has a party for everyone who will be part of the wedding party on the day – provided they are female, that is. This will mainly be for the benefit of the bridesmaids, but the mothers of bride and groom are often invited as well. This is a transatlantic custom that could well be transplanted here; it is an ideal way for the bridesmaids to meet each other and for the mothers to relax before the pressures of the big day, and gives the bride an opportunity to stop organising things and enjoy herself with her friends.

Bridal showers are traditional in America, too; these are parties given by close friends of the bride where each guest brings some small item to help the bride set up home. These are often practical, prosaic things that might not feature on a conventional wedding list – things such as an eggtimer, pair of tights, a cookery book, tins or packets for the storecupboard, a bulletin board, etc. The shower may be held on one theme, for instance a kitchen shower or a garden shower.

In Germany an 'eve of the wedding' party can be held one or a few nights before the marriage. The guests are supposed to make as much noise as possible – accomplished by the clanging of saucepans, breaking of crockery, blowing of car horns, etc!

Joint parties

Some couples like to host an evening or lunchtime when both sets of parents can join them; this is a particularly good idea if the parents haven't met before. Some couples club together and take all four parents out for a meal, or simply have a get-together at one of the parents' homes.

If the groom's parents are having to travel quite a way to the bride's home town and stay overnight for one or more nights before the wedding, it is courteous for the bride's family to entertain them for a meal. This could be at the bride's home or it could be at a restaurant – the latter will probably produce less trouble for the bride's overworked mother, but might stretch the purse-strings even tighter in the process!

Pre-wedding parties – Checklists

Party checklists

If you decide to have a pre-wedding party or parties, use these checklists to help you sort out the details. The address sections will help your best man or friends to make sure that everyone that should be invited has been.

Groom's party

Guest	Address	Accepted

Bride's party

Guest	Address	Accepted

Bride's dress

The dress

Your wedding dress is probably the detail of your wedding that will take the most time and care to sort out – and will also be the detail that everyone else wants to know about. It will probably be the most expensive garment you will ever invest in, and will be crucial to your feeling of happiness and well-being on your wedding day. So take your time over every detail and don't let anyone rush you.

* * *

Traditions

The setting aside of a special dress to be worn only on the wedding day is a relatively recent custom; for many centuries ordinary brides were simply married in their smartest clothes. Often the only thing that distinguished a bride from all the other women at the wedding was that her hair was loose; this would be the last time that she would wear her hair 'down' as opposed to piled on top of her head, so she would make the most of the occasion by releasing it from its customary plaits or ponytail. For many years strict clothing rules governed who could wear what, so ordinary people were often barred from wearing special fabrics or garments.

Coloured dresses

In Roman times the traditional wedding colour was yellow; the bride wore a long yellow veil that covered her literally from head to foot. Different countries have different traditions for bridal wear; among cultures where the national costume is very elaborate and colourful, the bridal clothes are often simply extra-fine examples of the traditional skills of weaving and embroidery. For quite a few centuries silver was the colour for royal brides in this country, later followed by silver and white – this tradition has led to the custom of having silver accessories, such as bag and shoes, for the bride.

Ordinary brides knew that they would probably have to wear their wedding dress as their 'Sunday best' for several years to come, as they couldn't afford to splash out on two new outfits; dresses were often pale pink, yellow or blue, or even bright red. During the 17th century British families who had emigrated to America sent home for fabric from England for their wedding dresses; far from plain white or pastel fabrics, the most commonly chosen materials were brightly coloured and patterned. Blue was often a popular colour with brides in Britain as it was the traditional colour for the Virgin Mary's robe in paintings, and it also denotes constancy. Black and purple are the traditional colours of mourning and so were generally avoided, while green was considered unlucky.

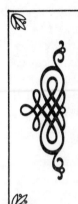

Which colour?

Married in white, you have chosen aright.
Married in green, ashamed to be seen.
Married in grey, you will go far away.
Married in red, you will wish yourself dead.
Married in blue, love ever true.
Married in yellow, ashamed of your fellow.
Married in black, you will wish yourself back.
Married in pink, your spirits will sink.
Married in brown, you'll live out of town.
Married in pearl, you'll live in a whirl.

The white wedding

The white wedding is a relatively recent innovation, although white has been associated with virginity and innocence since Elizabethan times. It was really Queen Victoria who started the cult of the white wedding on her marriage to Prince Albert; she broke with the tradition of royal brides wearing silver and chose white instead, and was slavishly followed throughout the land. The custom of white for the bride has never really died out since, although in recent years there has been a move towards introducing different colours to a basically white dress, for instance with the use of flowers, ribbons or embroidery in pale or bright colours. Many brides still choose white, but there is no reason at all why you shouldn't have another colour if you prefer. Cream and silver are two close alternatives to white if you don't want to move right away from tradition.

A description of an 18th century Quaker bride paints a very different picture from the austere image often associated with that group. The bride wore a light blue brocade dress with matching shoes (with very high heels), a short blue bodice, a white satin stomacher embroidered in multicoloured threads, and a black hood lined with white silk. Her groom, incidentally, was dressed in peachblossom cloth lined with quilted white silk.

Bride's dress – Where to obtain it

Buying, hiring or making?

One big question that needs to be answered near the beginning is – where are you going to obtain your dress? Will it be bought, made by you, made by a dressmaker, borrowed, hired? Cost may well be a factor in your choice. If you have little money to spare you will need to borrow or hire a dress, or have one made very cheaply. If you can spend a medium amount you could hire or make the dress, or buy one from a cheaper range or choose a secondhand gown. If you have a lot of money to spare the world is your oyster; you can have a dress made with all the frills and furbelows you care for, or you can buy the dress of your dreams.

Making it yourself

Some brides would never dream of buying a dress; they may have planned their own design, or maybe they know that they would never be able to buy quite the dress that they want, or at least not in the right fabric. Don't attempt to make your own wedding dress unless you are a very experienced dressmaker and totally at home with the fabric you choose and the techniques required. Paper patterns are available for wedding dresses, or you could adapt any other suitable dress pattern if you particularly like its neckline, waistline, etc; alternatively you can design the entire pattern yourself.

Whichever way you choose, it is worth taking the trouble to make a 'dummy' dress in cheap fabric first; that way you can adjust the size, fit, length, etc, and alter any details that don't please you before you cut into the expensive fabric. Make sure that you have all the right equipment for dealing with the fabric you choose – for instance long, fine pins for fitting, or the right needles and threads if the fabric is very delicate. Some brides combine the satisfaction of making their own dress with the reassurance of having the work done by a professional – they buy wedding dress kits that are cut out and ready to sew. Ask a friend or relation who is an experienced dressmaker to help you with the final fittings; it is impossible for you to perfect the fit on yourself or on a tailor's dummy.

Having your dress made by someone else

Brides who cannot buy what they want but who don't know one end of a needle from another need not despair: it is possible to get your dress made up by a

friend or relation, or by a professional dressmaker. They can use a commercial paper pattern or design a pattern to your specifications, and will be able to advise you on fabrics, styles, costs and trimmings. Don't be afraid to stick your neck out over the details and the fit: it is your dress, and you have the right to have it exactly as you want it. If your dress is being made up by a professional dressmaker, it is worth obtaining a written guarantee that the dress will be ready by the agreed date. Ask how many fittings will be required, and make sure that you attend them; some dressmakers will come to your house for fittings, while others prefer that you go to them.

Borrowing

Borrowing is certainly a cheap way out of the wedding dress problem, but only worth doing if a friend or relations has exactly the dress that you would love to wear. It is traditional in some parts of America for a daughter to wear her mother's wedding dress, but of course this only works if the two women are similar in size, shape, height and taste.

Buying

Many brides choose to buy their wedding dress, either new or secondhand, and any peep at a bridal magazine will show you the wealth of choice available. Many large stores have their own bridal room, and some shops are devoted exclusively to bridal wear; in these places you can browse at your leisure and try on as many styles as you want without any obligation to buy. It's a good idea to take someone with you whose judgement you trust; traditionally this role is taken by the bride's mother, but that might not always be the best choice! If alterations are needed, check whether the shop will do them.

Hiring

If you want a really special dress without having to pay a really special price for it, hiring is probably the answer. Look in your phone directory and the local papers for firms, and get a written guarantee that the dress you want will be available on the day you want it. Check whether you can collect the dress early (for instance if you want it when you choose your accessories), and also whether you have to have it cleaned before you take it back.

Bride's dress – Choosing a style

Styles of dress

What kind of dress are you looking for? One that evokes a particular era, for instance Victorian, Edwardian, or 1920s – or one that is in a particular mood, such as romantic, classic, elegant, severe? Whether you are buying, making or hiring your dress, choose a style that suits the tone of your wedding and is flattering to your figure.

1 Peasant style, with a laced bodice, puffed and gathered sleeves and a layered, gathered skirt.

2 American style, with ruffled sailor collar, bows at chest and sleeves, half-length gathered sleeves and calf-length gathered skirt.

3 Edwardian style, with high neckline, leg-of-mutton sleeves, fluted skirt with deep sash dropping below waist level.

4 1920s style, with dropped waist, very low back, plain neckline, and tight sleeves ending in a V over the hand, and three-quarter length skirt.

5 Pre-Raphaelite style, with layered ruffles on neck, sleeves skirt and waistband, scoop neckline and fully gathered skirt.

6 Jacobean style with tight bodice, low neckline with half-length puffed sleeves, full gathered skirt with flounces.

Bride's dress – Choosing a style

7 Mediaeval style, with high waist, centre-panelled bodice, square neckline, long angel sleeves and loose, swirling skirt.
8 Victorian style with full sleeves puffed at the shoulders and gathered into tight, ruffled cuffs, panelled bodice with high neckline, tight sash and full skirt with ruffles at the hem.
9 Tudor style, with box-pleated ruffles at neck and waist, V-pointed waistline, loose sleeves gathered at the elbows, lace trimmings and full plain skirt.

10 1950s style short satin dress with gathered skirt falling just below the knee, boat neckline, wide sash with bow, and no sleeves.

11 Classic style in princess line with a high waist, plain A-line skirt with half-train, plain neckline and straight sleeves.

12 Slim elegance with a gently gathered straight skirt, net bodice and sleeves over strapless top, sash and bow at waist.

10   11   12

Bride's dress – Finishing touches

Making your dress special

Once you have decided on the basic shape you want your dress to have, there are all kinds of embellishments that can be used on bought and home-made dresses that make that particular garment special. Some of the finishing touches are shown here; there are endless combinations of effect and colour.

1 Tiny coloured flowers can be dotted over the dress or over the hemline and sleeves.

2 Larger flowers can be made out of fabric and appliquéd to the dress.

3 Lace can be used for necklines and inset panels.

4 Ribbons can be used as sashes and to tie in bows on sleeves and flounces.

5 Ruffles of lace or fabric can be used to decorate sleeves, necklines, flounces or hemlines.

6 Small or large tucks can be made in the fabric of skirt, bodice or sleeve.

7 Embroidery can be used to decorate any part of the dress.

8 Net may be layered over the main fabric of the dress to give an ethereal look.

9 Flounces are real or pretend gatherings of the fabric, usually decorated with a bow.

10 Transparent lace may be used as a bodice and sleeve material over a more opaque fabric.

11 Sashes of any material can be used to nip in the waist and neaten the waistline.

12 Trains are extensions of the fabric at the back of the skirt; they are generally reserved for formal weddings.

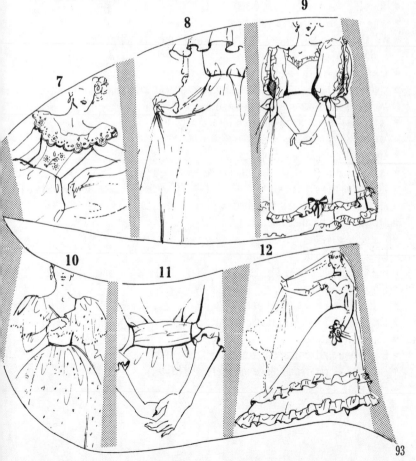

Bride's dress – Trying on/Checklist

Trying on

When you are trying on your dress, whether it is being made or whether you are just browsing in a shop, it is important that the fit is just right and that you feel completely happy in the garment. Here are some pointers to watch for.

- Does the dress look nice? (After all, you are going to be the centrepiece of the wedding ceremony.)
- Is it in the style that you want?
- Can you move your arms freely, or is it tight at the underarms or wrists?
- Can you breathe? (Remember that you will be wearing the dress for quite a few hours.)
- Does it fit well at the bodice and waist?
- Does it fit properly over your bust?
- Will the fit be spoilt if you lose or gain a few pounds before the wedding?
- Are the sleeves the right length?
- Is the hem the right length? (Remember to wear shoes similar to your wedding shoes when trying on the dress.)
- Is the neckline smooth and well-fitting?
- Are the seams finished neatly?
- Are all threads fastened off neatly?
- Is the zip put in straight and unobtrusively?
- How does the dress look from the back? (Through the ceremony all that most people will see is your back view.)
- Are any buttons attached firmly?
- Will it be easy to iron?
- Does it have to be dry–cleaned?
- Are any alterations needed?
- If so, who will do them, and how quickly?
- Is there any charge for alterations?
- Last but not least, how much does it cost?
- Can I afford it?
- Do I like it better than other dresses I have seen?
- Does it feel right, and make me feel like a bride?
- Do I want it?

Checklist for your wedding dress

Ask yourself these questions, and it will help you to decide just what kind of dress it is that you are looking for.

What is the mood of our wedding – formal or informal?	Do I want ruffles or flounces on any part of the dress?
What style of dress do I want to match this mood?	Do I want flowers at the neck, on the bodice or skirt, or on the sleeves?
Do I want a dress that reflects any particular era?	Do I want ribbons or bows anywhere?
What length skirt should it have?	Do I want a sash?
Will it have a train?	If so, how wide?
What kind of fabric would I prefer?	Should the sash be made of the dress fabric or something else?
What kind of waistline would I like?	How do I want the skirt and hemline trimmed?
Do I want the skirt flared, gathered or straight?	What colour dress do I want?
Do I want long, short, elbow-length or no sleeves?	Would I prefer cream or silver to white?
Should the sleeves have cuffs, bands or elastic?	Do I want any coloured ribbons or flowers on the dress?
Should the sleeves be straight, full, leg-of-mutton?	Do I want any embroidery on the dress?
Do I want the bodice fitted or loose?	Will it be easy to obtain or make bridesmaids' dresses to complement the style I want?
What kind of neckline am I looking for?	Will it be easy to obtain or make flower girls' dresses to complement the style I want?

Headdress

Headdresses

What am I going to wear on my head? This is perhaps the first question to ask once you have decided on your wedding dress. Of course you don't need to wear anything, but it is the rare bride who doesn't at least want to put a flower in her hair for the trip down the aisle.

The veil is the most traditional bridal headdress; it is seen in various forms in different cultures, where it sometimes had the purpose of preventing the bride and groom from seeing each other, and sometimes was supposed to offer symbolic protection to the couple. At times the veil was a piece of fabric held over the head of the bride or of the couple as the ceremony took place; in some cultures the bride was draped to the ground in the veil. Veils disappeared from fashion in this country for several centuries and brides tended to wear flowers instead; the joint Victorian cults of the white wedding and the coy female led to the reinstatement of the veil as a means of hiding the bride's supposed blushes!

1 Frothy veil decorated at the edges.
2 Lace veil worn to fringe the face.
3 Tulle veil piled high over the headdress.
4 Circular veil edged with ribbon.
5 Long tulle veil held in place with a tiara.
6 Full-length decorated veil.

Veils can be of many kinds, fabrics and lengths; generally they are of a transparent or semi-transparent material such as tulle or lace. They may be chosen so that they can be piled decoratively on top of the head or so that they fall smoothly down, and they may be held in place with a tiara, comb, clip or other headdress. Some veils are heirlooms and are worn by succeeding members of the family; these veils may be of very fine Brussels or Honiton lace, or may have been made by the original wearer.

*

In Ireland the ancient custom of holding the bride's veil in place with a sprig of mistletoe or a twig of hawthorn is still sometimes followed.

Headdress – Hats and circlets

Hats and circlets

Many brides choose to wear something other than a veil on their head, especially if the wedding is not very formal. Some of the many options are shown here.

1 Circlet bound in white ribbon and trimmed with ribbons and imitation flowers.

2 Round brimmed hat with a net of coarse tulle at the back.

3 Circlet of lace bows interspersed with imitation flowers and with a small lace veil.

4 Pointed circlet of white rings and imitation flowers.

5 Small flat hat with pearl-studded veil covering the face.

6 Tiara of imitation gemstones and flowers.

7 Wide-brimmed hat trimmed with net and ribbon.

8 Cap trimmed with ribbon and coarse veiling.

9 Flower and ribbon circlet holding a fall of lace.

Headdress – Using flowers

Floral headdresses

Flowers are very attractive as headdresses for your wedding; they can be used in many different ways, from single blooms to entire garlands. The flowers may be real or imitation; if you want to use real flowers in your hair on the day check the details with the florist when you order your bouquet.

1 White side comb holding trailing strands of tiny flowers.
2 Circlet of white and coloured flowers round a topknot.
3 Exotic-looking wreath of large net flowers and leaves.
4 Floral headdress holding a veil in place.
5 Circlet of large and small silk roses and coloured ribbons.

6 Ivory rose and rose petals decorating a chignon.
7 Wreath of white lilies.
8 Circlet of coloured flowers and ribbons.

9 Half-circlet of white and coloured roses and stephanotis.
10 Circlet of tiny flowers with star-shaped trim.
11 Side spray of flowers and stems.

Accessories

Accessories

It's no good choosing your dress carefully unless you pay just as much attention to what goes with it! Your accessories should complement the mood and style of your dress and of the wedding in general – for instance it would be inappropriate to wear flat white sandals with a very formal dress with a train. Keep your dress in mind when choosing all your accessories – ideally try them on with it – and you can be sure that the complete effect will be harmonious.

* * *

Shoes

You may not think that your shoes are particularly important, but they could make or break your wedding day. Choose shoes that are a sensible height so that you don't fall over when you are walking down the aisle or the church steps. Remember that you will be standing up for quite a long time during the day, so choose shoes that are comfortable. Try your shoes on with your dress to check that the hemline of the dress is not too short or too long. If your dress is full-length the hemline should barely brush the ground; anything longer is just asking for trouble! Shoes are generally white or silver to go with a white dress. When you are getting dressed on the big day, put your shoes on after your dress so that you don't rip the fabric as you get dressed.

Stockings

Decide in advance whether you want to wear white or neutral-coloured stockings or tights, and then buy two pairs in case of accidents! If your wedding is in the spring or autumn you may want to invest in a pair of warmer tights as a back-up in case the day dawns gloomy and cold.

Garter

It is traditional for brides to wear a garter in memory of the days when an unseemly scramble to remove the bride's garters was all part and parcel of the wedding celebrations...you may wish to dispense with this custom! If not, garters can be bought singly or in pairs.

In Germany many brides still save one-pfennig pieces to buy their shoes in accordance with an old tradtion. British brides used to slip a sixpence into one shoe before the ceremony.

*

Shoes have often played an important part in wedding ceremonies. In traditional Greek weddings the bride's mother stops the bride at the church door and asks her three times, 'Bride, has thou thy shoes?'

Coverings

It is not terribly appropriate to put a coat on over a wedding dress, which causes problems if the weather is cold or wet. It may be advisable to invest in a lacy but warm white shawl or one made of fringed or embroidered white fabric to put round your shoulders without spoiling the look of your dress if your wedding day is colder than anticipated. White parasols are more ornamental than useful, but photographers and wedding car chauffeurs may bring more practical white umbrellas with them; check this with the firms concerned.

When the bride and groom's first night, or 'bedding', was a much more public affair than nowadays, all kinds of frivolities were indulged in by the wedding guests. One of the traditions was that of 'flinging the stocking'; the bride's stockings were (forcibly) removed, then the guests would take it in turns to sit on the end of the bed and fling the stocking over their shoulder onto the bed, trying to get it to land on the groom (if the guest was male) or on the bride (if the guest was female).

Lingerie

Surprisingly, your lingerie can be a very important part of your wedding outfit. Once again you need to be comfortable, and you need a bra that is in no danger of riding up or coming undone. Try your bra and panties on under your dress: are there any unsightly lines or bulges? Can your underwear be seen under your dress? If so, what sort of petticoat will you need? Is the skirt of your dress full enough to warrant a stiff petticoat? If so you will find it much cheaper to order one through one of the bridal magazines than to buy one from a bridal shop.

Jewellery

Your jewellery should, of course, be chosen to complement your dress – for instance you will only be able to wear a pearl necklace or sparkling pendant if your dress has a low neckline or a plain high one. Earrings, too, should be tried on with your dress, and with your hair and headdress as you plan to have them on the day. Try all the jewellery you are thinking of wearing together with the dress itself – pearls might look too creamy, glittery necklaces too ornate.

In some parts of Austria the bride is presented with a 'tear-kerchief' woven of the finest linen; this is for drying the tears that she is presumed to shed on leaving home.

Checklist for bride's outfit

Dress

Is the dress laid out flat, not hanging up? (The fabric may be so heavy that it will pull the dress out of shape if left on a hanger.)	What am I going to do with the dress after I have changed?
Do I know how to iron the dress ready for the day?	If the dress is hired, who is going to clean and return it?
Have I tried it on for fit a few days before the wedding, to make sure I haven't gained or lost weight since it was chosen?	
Am I happy with the length?	Do I have an emergency repair kit at hand, in case of accidents?

Headdress

Have I tried on the headdress with the dress, to make sure that they complement one another?	How am I going to fix the headdress to my head? Do I need to buy any clips, bands or combs?
Have I tried on the headdress with the hairstyle I will have on the day?	How do I get any creases out of my veil?
Is it packed carefully so that it will not get crushed or mis-shapen?	
	If I am having real flowers, when do I need to collect them?
Do I need to buy any extra ribbons or flowers to go with it?	Have I double-checked the order with the florist?

Jewellery

Is all my jewellery ready?	What is going to happen to it when I change?
Does it all go together?	Are all the clasps and fastenings secure?
Does it all go with my dress?	Is it all clean and bright?

Shoes

Are my shoes the right height for my dress?	Are they clean?
Are they comfortable?	
	Have I removed all the labels from the soles?
Are they easy to walk in?	
	Have I broken them in so that they don't chafe?
Are the soles non-slip?	

Stockings

Have I got a clean new pair of stockings or tights?	Do I need a thick pair of tights in case of cold weather?
Have I got a back-up pair?	

Underwear

Does my bra make a good line under my dress?	Do I need a petticoat to make my skirt stand out?
Does any of my bra show above my neckline?	Are my undies comfortable?
Can you see my undies through my dress?	Are they right for the weather – cool in summer, warm in winter?

Miscellaneous

Do I want a parasol?	Do I want to go for 'something old, something new, something borrowed, something blue'? If so, what?
Do I want a shawl?	
Where am I going to keep my handkerchief?	
What happens if it rains or is cold?	Should I be wearing any family heirlooms?

Looking your best

❀❀❀❀❀❀❀❀❀❀❀❀

Looking your best

Needless to say, on your wedding day you will want to look your very best, with all your good points emphasised and your weaker points played down. Go over in your mind each aspect of your appearance – weight, complexion, hair, make-up, etc – and think it through in the light of how you want to look on your wedding day.

***

Face

A good deal of attention will be focused on your face, as this is the focus of your general wellbeing and emotions – and also the cause of lots of beauty problems! However, with a little planning and preparation you will be able to be a radiant bride. Even if you don't generally wear very much make-up, make an exception for your wedding day; with all the finery around you it is easy for your face to 'disappear' and be overshadowed. Plan to wear quite a lot of well-chosen and well-applied foundation, blusher, eye-shadow and lipstick, and choose colours that tone well with your skin tones, your dress, and the flowers you will be carrying. Check, too, that the colours match your going-away outfit; there won't be time for a total reworking while you are changing at the reception.

There may be aspects of your appearance that you would like to camouflage a little for the special day, even if you are not usually too bothered about them. Moles and prominent birthmarks can be covered with special cosmetics; beauticians will be able to advise you on choosing and applying suitable preparations. Unwanted hair can be bleached, if it is fine, or removed by electrolysis if it is dark or coarse, and eyebrows can be plucked into the chosen shape. If you plan any hair removal by plucking or electrolysis, schedule this for at least a week before the wedding in case any redness or soreness results. Spots afflict almost everyone at some time; buy an antiseptic cover stick to match your skin tone well before the wedding, so that you are prepared for emergencies on the day!

Facials are a wonderful way of bringing a healthy glow to your skin; defoliants remove rough and dead skin cells to leave your skin looking clearer, and face masks bring impurities to the surface so that they can be sloughed off by the skin's cleansing processes. Tanning makes your skin look brown and healthy, and also helps to get rid of acne, but you need to keep your skin moisturised so that it doesn't dry out. Saunas can make you feel extra clean and glowing with health, as can mud baths and massage. If

you plan saunas, tanning sessions or other radical health treatments in preparation for your wedding, book them at least a week before the date so that your body has time to readjust and even out any excesses. Facials will be most effective if done the day before your wedding.

Hair

You will want your hair to look at its best for your wedding, and this will involve quite a bit of forward planning. The condition of your hair will be improved enormously if you are eating a good diet and getting plenty of fresh air and exercise and healthy food for some months before your wedding – and your face will look at its best too.

You will need to choose a hairstyle for the day that suits the general shape of your face and body, goes with the feel of your outfit (for instance, you don't want punk spikes with a romantic flounced gown), and will suit the headdress you have chosen. Just before your wedding is not a good time to make radical changes in the cut or colour of your hair – there won't be enough time for it to revert if you decide you don't like the result! Take your headdress along to your hairdresser, or try it out yourself, some weeks before the actual wedding day, so that you can get all the details sorted out in good time. Make sure that the style and headdress feel secure, and also that you will be able to adapt the style to suit your going-away outfit.

Hands

There will also be quite a lot of attention paid to your hands, as everyone will be wanting to look at your new wedding ring. Give your hands a good manicure in the week before your wedding, moisturising them and shaping the nails well and rubbing in plenty of cream. Then you will be ready for your final application of nail varnish, if you are wearing it, and hand cream on the day.

Weight

If you need to lose some weight before your wedding – start early, and take it slowly. Don't leave it to the last minute; either you will never manage to diet in the middle of all the preparations, or you will be tempted to follow an unhealthy crash diet. Lose the weight slowly and sensibly and then it is more likely to stay off. If you are in any doubt as to what foods to eat to lose weight, ask your doctor or join a slimming group; losing weight alongside other people often adds that extra impetus needed for the diet to succeed.

Bridesmaids' dresses

Bridesmaids

Virtually everything that applies to the making, buying or hiring of the bride's dress applies also to the bridesmaids' dresses; it is important that each bridesmaid feels completely happy with her outfit on the big day. Often bridesmaids live in different towns from one another or from the bride, so getting all the outfits ready simultaneously may prove quite tricky. Start early to ensure that there is enough time to do all the dresses properly.

* * *

Colours

What colours are your bridesmaids going to wear? This can be quite a difficult choice; you want a basic colour that blends well with your dress and with the flowers that you want to carry, that coordinates with the clothes that will be worn by the rest of the wedding party, and that suits the ages, colourings and personal preferences of the bridesmaids themselves. It is only kind to consult the bridesmaids about the choice of colour, especially if they are contributing towards the cost of the outfit themselves.

The traditional colours for bridesmaids' outfits are the pastels – yellow, lilac, pink, pale blue, peach. Green used to be considered unlucky, but green can be a very pretty colour indeed for bridesmaids' clothes. However, there is no need at all to stick to pastel colours. Darker violet, beige, brown, vivid pink, red, midnight blue, turquoise; all these could look very attractive on bridesmaids of the right colouring. Also there is no need to choose a plain colour; the dresses can be in a check, a print, stripes, spotted material, etc, or in a mixture of fabrics, for instance a plain bodice with patterned skirt and sleeves. Or the skirts could be made of one colour with a flounced or shorter overskirt in another colour.

If the colouring of your bridesmaids is very different, for instance if one has jet-black hair and coffee-coloured skin while the other has reddish blonde hair and a peaches-and-cream complexion, make very sure that your chosen colour suits them both! If the bridesmaids are of very different ages you may want to dress them in two tones of the same basic colour, for instance a plain blue dress for the matron of honour and a blue and white print for the junior bridesmaid.

Styles

You will also need to choose a style of dress that suits all your bridesmaids. For instance, it may be quite appropriate to dress a six-year-old girl in a short

dress, white pantaloons and a mob cap, but this would not look so good on a
35-year-old matron of honour! Similarly, low-necked off-the-shoulder dresses
look fine on older bridesmaids with good figures but would look inappropriate
on small girls.

You may want to choose a basic style of dress that reflects the pattern of your
wedding dress. This will help to give an overall homogeneity to the bridal
party. Many ranges of off-the-peg bridal gowns have coordinating bridesmaids'
dresses available to complement them, and many sew-it-yourself patterns
either have sister patterns for bridesmaids' dresses or give instructions for
making attendants' dresses from the main bridal gown shape. Obviously this
only works if your bridesmaids are the same size and shape as you are.
If your bridesmaids cover a wide age range, you can probably think up
adaptations of a basic dress pattern that would suit all of the different ages.
For instance, the basic pattern could be a style with a fitted bodice and a
gathered skirt. The matron of honour and any older bridesmaids could wear
dresses with low necks and off-the shoulder sleeves; teenage bridesmaids
could wear the basic pattern with a scoop neck and puffed sleeves, and
younger bridesmaids could wear dresses with a high neck and puffed sleeves.
The younger bridesmaids' hems could be knee-length instead of full-length.

For very young bridesmaids it is always sensible to keep away from
floor-length hems; it is very easy for a small girl to trip over a long hem. Make
the dress ankle-length, calf-length or knee-length. If your bridesmaids are
very different shapes, make sure that you find a pattern that flatters them all.
A heavy bridesmaid will feel ridiculous in a closely fitted and gathered dress,
especially if she is with sylph-like counterparts.

Bridesmaids' dresses – Fabrics/ Accessories/Checklist

Fabrics

During the 50s and 60s satins were the rule for bridesmaids' dresses, and were very suitable for the extremely simple princess styles and straight skirts of those eras. Since the advent of 'flower power' and subsequent fashion trends, dresses for both bride and bridesmaids have become much more feminine. As a result many more fabrics have been brought into use for bridesmaids' dresses – prints, ginghams, cottons, slubbed silks, broderie anglaise, checks, etc. Choose a fabric that complements your wedding dress; for instance if you are all layers and layers of fine net and organdie, bridesmaids in tartan wouldn't look very appropriate – or if you are in Edwardian style, bridesmaids in satin and net crinolines would look strange. Don't just look in the 'bridal' departments of shops for fabrics and dresses; these tend to be very safe and predictable. Shop around in boutiques and the other departments, and you could come across just what you are looking for.

Accessories

Once again it is best to have accessories that complement your own in style; the bridesmaids' bouquets, headdresses and shoes should all echo your own rather than clash with them. Shoes for older bridesmaids could be sandals, court shoes or satin slippers; shoes for younger bridesmaids could be pale party shoes or ballet slippers, or even patent leather shoes in a pretty style. As with your own shoes, make sure that all those of your attendants are non-slip!

In America, dogs have been used as wedding attendants and dyed to match the bride's colour scheme!

*

The women attending the bride in Roman times were married, but in Anglo-Saxon Britain the tradition grew for the attendants to be unmarried.

*

In traditional Korean and Japanese weddings there are no bridesmaids, but the bride is attended by an elderly woman.

Checklist for bridesmaids' clothes

Who are my bridesmaids going to be?	What fabric will be suitable?
	Should the fabric be plain or patterned?
	Do we want any extra design features, such as tucks, bows, sashes, ribbons, flowers, frills, overskirts, aprons, etc?
What colour(s) will they be wearing?	What headdresses will they wear?
Will this blend in with the rest of the wedding party?	
Will their dresses reflect mine in style?	What shoes will they wear?
Will they be bought, made or hired?	
If made, who will make them? Will the same person make them all?	What colour tights or socks will they wear?
Is there a chief bridesmaid?	
If so, how will she be distinguished?	What jewellery will they wear with the dresses?
Is the style flattering to all my bridesmaids?	
Does the colour chosen suit them all?	When will the dresses be ready?
Can they all wear the same style of dress?	
If not, how can we adapt the basic style?	Who will look after the dresses until the day?
What length will the dresses be?	Where will the bridesmaids dress for the wedding?

Bridesmaids' dresses – Optional styles

Styles for bridesmaids' dresses
Bridesmaids' dresses can come in
almost any shape and colour; the
styles shown here are just some of
the many options.

1 Formal plain satin
dress with fitted bodice,
puffed and gathered
sleeves and gently
gathered skirt.

2 Ruffled dress with
sash and puffed sleeves.

3 Gingham dress with
broderie anglaise apron
and mob cap.

4 Ruffled and frilled dress that could be made up in a plain or printed fabric.

5 Striped dress with leg-of-mutton sleeves and square neckline.

6 White dress with sash and underskirt in a contrasting colour.

Bridesmaids' dresses – Optional styles

7 Bride's and bridesmaid's dresses showing how the same basic style can be adapted. The bride's dress has flowers along the neck ruffle and skirt, and a gathered overskirt that has been caught up with ribbons. The bridesmaid's dress has a narrower neck frill and ruffle around the skirt.

8 Dresses for two bridesmaids of very different ages, made up in two shades of peach. Both dresses have gathered and ruffled sleeves and are trimmed with lace.

9 Matching bridesmaids' dresses in white overlaid with spotted voile; these dresses would suit bridesmaids of any age from young girls to a matron of honour.

Flower girls' dresses

Flower girls

If you have a very small sister, niece, cousin, etc, you may want to have her in your wedding party as a flower girl. This role could be purely decorative – she could be chosen just to look pretty and add some variety to the attendants – or you could detail her to precede the bride down the aisle scattering flower petals or confetti. Of course, you will need to check this with the church caretaker before the event!

If you have a flower girl as well as bridesmaids, her outfit should in some way be distinctive so that she doesn't appear to be just another bridesmaid. Her dress could be in the same fabric as the others but made up in a different style, for instance shorter with pantaloons, or smocked with puff sleeves instead of low-necked with a fitted bodice. Alternatively she could wear a dress that is quite different but still toning; if the bridesmaids are in peach she

could wear a peach and cream print, for example, or if they are in a yellow and green flower print she could wear a pretty dress in plain yellow or pale green.

Shown here are some styles that would be eminently suitable for a small flower girl.

1 Peasant style, with gathered skirt, checkered overskirt, white puff-sleeve blouse and black waistcoat.

2 Party dress with tucked sleeves and hemline, wide sash and pantaloons.

3 Layered white dress with trails of flowers from the sleeves and overskirt.

4 Smocked dress with puffed sleeves and ribbon decoration.

Pageboys' outfits

Pageboys' clothes
These styles show a selection of the outfits that could be chosen for a pageboy or pageboys..

1 Velvet jacket and grey trousers with bow tie.
2 Morning suit complete with wing collar and top hat.
3 Traditional velvet knickerbocker suit.
4 Formal suit with striped trousers and waistcoat.
5 Bellhop's outfit.
6 Scottish outfit including kilt and sporran.
7 Sailor suit.

2

3

6

7

119

Groom's clothes

Groom and other men

It is easy for the groom's clothes to be forgotten in all the busy preparation and planning of the bride's outfit, but if she is looking her best it is important that she has a groom to do her justice! Also the groom sets the whole tone for the clothes of all the other men in the wedding party; if the groom wears a morning suit, so should the bride's father and the groom's father, the best man and any ushers. At a very formal wedding it might even be requested that all the male guests wear morning dress. If the groom and best man simply wear smart suits, that too will set the pattern for the other guests.

***

Accessories

You will need to decide first of all on what kind of suit you will wear, and once you have done that you can choose accessories to go with it. For instance, with a morning suit you have a choice of a plain collar and tie or a wing collar and stock; you could also choose top hats, gloves, and a matching or subtly contrasting waistcoat. You will also need to think about shoes and socks; black is generally the best choice if you are wearing black, grey or blue, but these days there are also many attractive men's styles available in grey and blue. If you are wearing a brown lounge suit, choose brown or beige shoes and socks to match. Think carefully about what kind of tie you want; it could be any colour from plain blue or grey to striped or quite brightly coloured.

Colour schemes

It is important to check that the colour scheme you choose for yourself and the best man tones well with the colours for the bride and bridesmaids. With a little forward planning it is possible to make sure that the whole wedding party is well coordinated. For instance, the bridesmaids could be in a red and white print, carrying red and white flowers, or in pink with red trimmings, and the men could wear grey or blue with red buttonholes or red ties. Or the bride could be in cream, the bridesmaids in yellow, carrying cream, yellow and peach flowers, and the groom and best man could wear brown or beige morning suits.

To hire or to buy?

You will need to sort out early on where you are going to get your wedding clothes. If you are wearing a lounge suit you have several options: you could wear one you already have; you could have a suit made; you could buy one off-the-peg; or you could hire one. Hire firms don't just do very formal clothes. If you choose to wear a morning suit you will almost certainly need to hire it; it is unlikely that you would wear one often enough to justify buying one at great expense. Check with the hire firm when you can collect the suit, when it needs to be returned, and whether it has to be cleaned before being returned.

Checklist for groom's clothes

Use this list to check that you have got all your clothes and accessories sorted out and ready for the big day.

Suit
Waistcoat
Shirt
Tie
Gloves
Top hat
Tiepin
Watch chain
Underpants
Shoes
Socks
Handkerchief
Cufflinks
Clothes for going away in

*At the weddings of the Hungarian Bessanyo people, the best man
used to wear an evergreen wreath on his head topped by a doll.
This supposedly symbolised the bridegroom's love for the bride.*

Groom's clothes – Choosing an outfit

Groom's clothes

Shown here are some options for the groom's outfit; the men of the wedding party should wear clothes of the same style and degree of formality or informality.

1 Lounge suit with waistcoat.
2 Morning suit with wing collar, stock and top hat.
3 Morning suit with ordinary collar and tie.

4 Morning suit with darker jacket and gloves.

5 Formal suit with dark jacket and striped waistcoat and trousers.

Groom's clothes – Choosing an outfit

6 For a formal afternoon wedding followed by an evening reception, a dinner jacket with cummerbund, tartan trews, dress shirt and bow tie.

7 White tie and tails – a short tail-jacket, stiff shirt, white bow tie and black top hat.

8 Outfit for the traditional wedding of a Scot.
9 Double-breasted suit.

10 Morning suit with dark jacket, pale waistcoat, top hat and striped trousers.

Mothers' clothes

The wedding of a daughter or a son is a very big day for their mother and she will want to look her very best. Many women buy or make a special outfit for their son's or daughter's wedding; they know that they will be in the public eye all day, so it is important to have an outfit that is comfortable, practical and smart. Many women opt for the classic combination of a smart suit and hat, but there are no hard and fast rules; a beautiful dress with no hat is perfectly acceptable, as is a skirt and

attractive blouse.

It is worthwhile for the mothers of the bride and groom to consult with the couple closely on colour schemes; the whole wedding party will be standing together and being photographed together for much of the day, so it is all to the good if everyone's outfit tones into an overall scheme.

These styles are just some of the outfits that would be eminently suitable for a daughter's or son's wedding.

Flowers

Flowers

Flowers have played a part in countless weddings throughout the centuries, and a wedding wouldn't really feel complete without them. In ancient Roman and Anglo-Saxon wedding ceremonies both the bride and the groom wore garlands, and in the Middle Ages children strewed flowers in the path of the bride as she emerged from the church – this is the origin of our tradition of the flower girl. In early rural weddings in this country the bridal wreath often consisted of ears of corn or wheat, signifying plenty and fertility, and in some traditions the bride still carries ears of grain in her bouquet.

***

Your flowers

Flowers for your wedding can be as simple or as elaborate as you choose; there is no set rule to follow. You may want to restrict them to a bouquet for yourself, particularly if you are going for a small, simple registry office wedding, or you may want to splash out on large bouquets for bride and bridesmaids, buttonholes for all the men, corsages for the bride's and groom's mother, elaborate arrangements for church and reception, and flowers around the cake. You will also need to decide who is going to do your flowers. Ask several different florists for quotations and examples of their work so that you can compare the service. You may decide that you want to use artificial silk flower arrangements – ask around for a specialist who can make them up for you.

Colour schemes

Choose the colours of all the flowers carefully so that they all blend together tastefully. You may want to have all white blooms in your bouquet; if so, remember that white flowers can look very yellow against a blue/white dress. Colours for flowers could be pastel, such as pale blue, violet, pale yellow or pink; they could be rich and dark such as purple, crimson, scarlet or deep peach; they could be autumnal such as gold, orange and beige, or they could be bright such as blue and yellow, red, white and green, flame, purple and gold. Make sure that they complement the complexions, hair colours and dress fabrics of you and your bridesmaids.

At American weddings in the 19th century it was traditional to have a large bridal bell made from white flowers hanging above the bride and groom as they were married.

Seasonal guide to flowers

Some flowers are only available at certain times of the year; others may be available when not in season but at a vastly inflated price. Check with the florist when you are comparing prices. Plenty of the most popular flowers for bouquets, such as carnations, irises, roses, freesias and lilies are available all the year round. Some blooms, such as lilacs, lilies of the valley, cornflowers, heathers, lilies, carnations, daisies and gladioli are particularly long-lasting, and will not wilt at the crucial time!

Winter flowers	Spring flowers	Summer flowers	Autumn flowers
Carnation	Azalea	Aster	Chrysanthemum
Chrysanthemum	Apple blossom	Azalea	Daisy
Freesias	Broom	Carnation	Dahlia
Forsythia	Bluebell	Cornflower	Freesia
Gypsophila	Carnation	Chrysanthemum	Gladioli
Gentian	Cherry blossom	Delphinium	Gypsophila
Iris	Chrysanthemum	Daisy	Hydrangea
Lily	Clematis	Freesia	Iris
Orchid	Camellia	Fuchsia	Lily
Rose	Daffodil	Gladioli	Morning-glory
Stephanotis	Daisy	Hollyhock	Orchid
Snowdrop	Forsythia	Heather	Rose
Winter jasmine	Freesia	Iris	
	Gladioli	Jasmine	
	Honeysuckle	Lilac	
	Iris	Lily	
	Jasmine	Lily of the valley	
	Lilac	Lupin	
	Lily	Marigold	
	Mimosa	Orchid	
	Orchid	Peony	
	Polyanthus	Rose	
	Rhododendron	Rhododendron	
	Stephanotis	Stock	
	Tulip	Sweet pea	
		Sweet William	
		Tiger lily	

Foliage

Bouquets often have a little greenery to offset the colour of the flowers, but most arrangements are so ornate that they don't need much. Popular choices are ivy, asparagus fern, lily of the valley leaves, myrtle and bracken.

Flowers – Bouquets

Bouquets

Bouquets come in many shapes and sizes, from the floor-to-shoulder draperies of lilies seen early this century to a single bloom carried by the bride. Most, though, are somewhere in the middle! When choosing the shape and size of your bouquet keep in mind your own height and build and colouring, the length and fabric of your dress, the 'feel' of the wedding – very formal, country garden, minimal ceremony, spring, winter, etc – and, last but not least, how much you want to spend.

1 Single bloom

2 Circular posy

3 Posy with ribbons

4 Large round bouquet

5 Spray of flowers

6 Teardrop or fall

7 Trailing teardrop

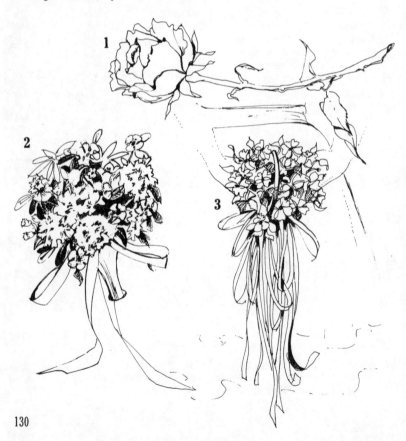

4

5

6

7

Flowers – A united effect

Other flowers

Flowers for your wedding are unlikely to stop at just your bouquet and flowers for the bridesmaids! You may want to continue the colour scheme of your flowers through to the buildings and the other guests so that they unite the whole day in your chosen colours.

Flower girls

In many countries of the world small children attend marriage or betrothal ceremonies and scatter flowers, so traditionally flower girls (usually aged under 10) carry baskets of flowers.

Buttonholes

These had their origins in the tradition of the men at the wedding wearing 'favours' – usually knots of ribbon – in the bride's chosen colours. In the 18th century the men wore flat white satin bows on their shoulders. These days the buttonholes are more likely to be carnations, roses or lilies of the valley. They can be ordered for just the men of the wedding party (groom, best man, pageboys, fathers of bride and groom) or for all the men who will be attending the wedding.

At the registry office

Many registry offices are decorated with fresh flowers in pretty arrangements each day, and so you may not need to provide them yourself. Check with the registrar when you make arrangements for your wedding.

At the church

Some churches have restrictions on the colours or sizes of the flowers allowed inside; check this in good time. Sometimes you can choose the flowers in conjunction with the person who would normally have been arranging the church flowers for the following Sunday – if so you may not need to pay all the cost of the flowers yourselves. Pew ends are decorative flower arrangements in the shape of posies, rings, hearts or sprays: this is an American custom that is becoming popular in this country as well.

At the reception

Flower arrangements at the reception will continue the festival air and brighten up even the dullest hall. If the reception is formal you could order a small arrangement for each table and larger ones for the sides of the room. For a buffet the tables could include a selection of small arrangements. The cake may be topped or surrounded by fresh flowers. Some brides and grooms arrange surprise bouquets for presentation to their mothers just before they leave for their honeymoon.

Elaborate Jewish weddings use a canopy of flowers in place of the fabric canopy (huppah) *used to cover the couple during the ceremony.*

One American custom for formal weddings is to ask the florist to make up centrepieces for the reception tables, with each centrepiece consisting of several small bouquets which can be given to the guests as they leave.

If you are having your wedding reception at the bride's home, why not make up a little flower arrangement for the door knocker, to welcome the guests as they arrive.

Flowers – Checklists/Meaning

Bride's flowers

What shape do I want my bouquet?	Do I need any fresh flowers for my hair or headdress?
What 'feel' do I want to give with the flowers I choose?	What colour flowers do I want?
Are there any favourite flowers I want included?	How much do I have available to spend on flowers?
	How early do I have to order from the florist?
If so, are they available at this time of year?	Will the flowers be delivered, or do I have to collect them?
Do I want to include any flowers because of their sentimental value?	Will the flowers be ready the night before the wedding or on the day?

Reception flowers

Will these be done by the caterer, if we have one?	What flower arrangements do we want – size, quantity, colours?
Will these be done by the restaurant or hotel holding the reception?	
How much will they charge?	Do we want any extra arrangements to decorate the tables or the cake?

The meaning of flowers
In Victorian times the 'language of flowers' was an elaborate code which lovers (or suitors) used to send detailed messages to each other. Here are the meanings of some of the flowers that you may wish to include in your bouquet.

Carnation fascination, love
Chrysanthemum, red I love
Chrysanthemum, white truth
Daffodil regard
Daisy innocence
Flowering almond hope
Fern fascination, sincerity
Forget-me-not remembrance
Heliotrope devotion, faithfulness

Honeysuckle generosity
Hyacinth, white loveliness
Ivy geranium bridal flower
Ivy fidelity, marriage
Iris flame, my compliments
Japonica, white loveliness
Jasmine amiability
Lemon blossom fidelity in love
Lilac, white youthful innocence
Lily, white purity, modesty

Attendants' flowers

What kind of bouquets do I want for the bridesmaids?	How many buttonholes do we need?
	Who will collect these, and when?
Do I want them the same colour as my bouquet, or different?	
	Who will hand them out, if the guests are to have buttonholes?
Will they be the same shape and size for each bridesmaid?	What colour buttonholes do we want?
	What flower do we want for the buttonholes?
What kind of arrangement does the flower girl need?	
	Do we want to order flowers for the mothers of the bride and groom?

Church/registry office flowers

Who will do these?	At what stage are the church flowers put in place?
Who will pay for them?	Do we want any pew ends or extra flowers?

For all your flowers, leave a contact phone number in case of emergencies, and phone several days before the wedding to check that all the details are correct.

Lily majesty
Lily of the valley return of happiness
Magnolia perseverance
Mimosa sensitivity
Maidenhair discretion
Orange blossom your purity equals your loveliness
Peach blossom captive
Pink boldness
Rose love, beauty
Rose, white I am worthy of you

Sweet pea delicate pleasures
Tulip, red love
Tulip, variegated beautiful eyes
Tulip, yellow hopeless love
Veronica fidelity
Violet faithfulness

And, finally, some messages you might **not** want to put in your bouquet!

Ill temper (barberry)
My regrets follow you to the grave (asphodel)
Anxious and trembling (red columbine)
Scandal (hellebore)
Chagrin (marigold)
I wish I were rich (kingcup)
My best days are past (meadow saffron)
Touch me not (burdock)

Gifts to give

Presents for others

As bride and groom you will want to show your appreciation to the people who have been involved in your wedding party, and the best way is by giving them a present to remind them of the special day. Try to make these presents lasting and, if possible, personal; they will like to have something that they can look at in later years, and something that has obviously been selected with care and thought.

***

Best man and ushers

It is often difficult to select presents for men, but some things are very suitable for men of the wedding party; these include cufflinks, decanters, tiepins, watches, engraved tankards, etc. You will want to give your best man something more special than the gifts you give to your ushers, as he will have done much more work for the big day! Of course you will know the personal tastes of your own best man and may well want to choose an unusual gift for him such as a brandy goblet, a leather jacket, a television, etc.

Bridesmaids

Bridesmaids are very much easier to choose presents for, as any kind of jewellery is appropriate and also any kind of beautiful ornament. Presents for bridesmaids could be necklaces, pendants, bracelets, rings, earrings, stick pins, engraved glasses or goblets, figurines, special thimbles, etc. Some couples choose jewellery for their bridesmaids that can be worn on the wedding day to complement the bridesmaids' dresses.

Other attendants

Flower girls and other small female attendants are also easy to choose presents for; they too could be given a pretty necklace or pendant, a figurine, or a pretty set of crockery such as the Beatrix Potter or Brambly Hedge designs. Little boys are harder to choose for, and it is difficult to think of many presents that small boys will be interested in for long; you may well find that the best bet is something like a computer game or a special toy. Some firms provide wedding dolls for small girls; you could vary this idea by dressing a doll in a replica of your own dress, or in a dress made from the same fabric as the attendant's.

***

In Uganda the Baganda people associate the banana plant with fertility, and on the arrangement of an approved marriage the bride's brother presents her with banana leaves.

Presents for each other

Although you will have been spending out a lot of money on the other preparations for your wedding, you will probably want to give each other something special as a gift to mark this special day. Your presents to each other will reflect your financial state, so don't feel obliged to give something showy if you can't afford it. If money is no object the groom could give the bride a string of pearls, a fur coat, a diamond pendant, a car; she could give him a motorbike, a subscription to a golf club, gold cufflinks, etc. Keep your ears and eyes open for clues to the presents that would really please your partner; the bride might be delighted with something more prosaic such as a guitar, a rocking chair or a cookery course, while the groom may hanker after a camera, a leather suitcase or a set of brandy glasses.

Parents

Some brides and grooms like to buy a small present for their parents as they finally leave home for the last time, to say 'thank you' for all their care over the years. Others choose a present for their respective mothers, such as a dish commemorating the day, an engraved perfume bottle or a piece of jewellery, or arrange to have a bouquet of flowers delivered on the day. Both sets of parents would be delighted with a wedding photograph in a silver or enamel frame.

Presents for everyone

In some countries it is customary for everyone at a wedding to take away a small favour – often sweets wrapped up prettily. Several wedding firms provide wedding favours such as boxes of dragées, lace squares enclosing sugared almonds, wedding crackers, and commemorative scrolls thanking the guest for attending.

* * *

Among Zulu tribes presents between bride and groom often took the form of beads; these were considered particularly special as they had actually been worn by the person concerned.

In some of the ancient Masai tribes the man seeking a particular girl's hand in marriage is given snuff and a meal of porridge by her father. The next day, and the day after that, he brings a present of beer for the father, and on the third day comes back with the dowry or bride-price in the shape of cattle or goats. On the fourth day he comes back again to claim his bride.

The service

What constitutes a marriage?

The word 'wedding' comes from the Anglo-Saxon word *wed*, meaning a pledge (especially a financial one), and it is this pledge, in its modern form, that constitutes a marriage. For the marriage to be legal in this country it has to take the form of a public declaration, before at least two adult witnesses, that the couple intend to live together as husband and wife, and know of no reason legally why they are not free to marry. They must also fulfil the legal requirements in every respect (see pp 22–27).

* * *

In Church of England services these requirements are bound up in the wording of the marriage ceremony. In ceremonies held at registry offices or in churches of other denominations, both parties must make a public declaration in these or similar words: 'I do solemnly declare that I know not of any lawful impediment why I (full name) may not be joined in matrimony to (full name of partner)'. Then each must say: 'I call upon these persons here present to witness that I (full name) do take thee (full name of partner) to be my lawful wedded wife/husband'.

In Egypt the marriage contract used to be arranged between the groom and the bride's deputy; they joined hands and the hands were then covered with a cloth to complete the union.

In Church of England ceremonies the vows taken before God are quite complex, involving the well-known phrases 'for better, for worse, for richer, for poorer, in sickness and in health, till death us do part'. These are solemn vows, not to be undertaken lightly; if you do not feel that you can honestly take them it is better to choose a marriage in a registry office rather than be hypocritical. If you are getting married in an Anglican ceremony you will find that the vicar will probably offer you the choice of several different versions of the marriage service; some are traditional, some modern. Choose the type that best suits the kind of vows you want to make and the tone of your wedding in general. In some ceremonies both inside and outside the Anglican church it is possible to write your own vows, so that you can phrase them to emphasise the things you both feel will be important in your marriage. Generally you will repeat the vows in small phrases after the minister, but it is possible to read your vows or to learn them, which can be very moving – but make sure that you have a crib sheet handy in case your mind goes blank!

When a Quaker wedding takes place, the groom holds the bride's hand and makes this declaration: 'Friends, I take this, my friend (name of bride) to be my wife, promising, through Divine assistance, to be unto her a loving and faithful husband so long as we both on Earth shall live.'

In one medieval wedding vow the wife promised to be 'debonair and buxom, in bed and at board'.

There are three elements that compose a marriage under Jewish tradition. The first is the groom's recitation of the wedding vow, an ancient Aramaic vow which when translated means 'Behold thou art consecrated unto me with this ring according to the law of Moses and of Israel'; he recites this as he places the ring on his bride's finger. The second element is the reading of the *ketubbah*, the legal marriage document which spells out the obligations and rights of the bride and groom. This is the Jewish equivalent of the marriage certificate, and is held as a treasured possession by the bride; the text reads along these lines:

'On the   th day of the week, the   nth day of the month of   , in the year   corresponding to the   of   , the holy covenant of marriage was entered into, in   , between the bridegroom   , and his bride,   . The said bridegroom made the following declaration to his bride; be thou my wife according to the law of Moses and of Israel. I faithfully promise that I will be a true husband unto thee. I will honour and cherish thee; I will work for thee; I will protect and support thee, and will provide all that is necessary for thy due sustenance, even as it beseemeth a Jewish husband to do. I also take upon myself all such further obligations for thy maintenance during thy lifetime as are prescribed by our religious statutes.

And the said bride plighted her troth unto him, in affection and with sincerity, and has thus taken upon herself the fulfilment of all the duties incumbent upon a Jewish wife. This covenant of marriage was duly executed and witnessed this day according to the usage of Israel'.

The third element that completes the marriage is the symbolic union, the *yihud*. After the recessional the bride and groom retire into a private room for a short time, where they have some food together; this is often a special wedding broth.

The service – Additional ceremonies

Additional ceremonies

As well as the legal aspect of marriage in this country, and the words that need to be repeated publicly before the marriage is valid, there are various ceremonies that have grown up around the traditional exchange of vows. One is the ceremony of the ring; in most cases the groom gives a ring to the bride, and in some cases she also gives a ring to the groom. These are placed on the 'ring finger' with appropriate sentiments, varying from tradition to tradition.

Another ceremony is that of giving the bride away. Traditionally it is the bride's father that performs this duty, a legacy of the times when marriages were financial contracts made for convenience rather than unions of love. The bride's father accompanies her down the aisle before the ceremony, stands just behind her at the front of the church, and indicates his assent when the minister says 'Who gives this woman to be married to this man?' or similar words. If the bride's father has died she can be given away by her uncle, brother, grandfather, godfather or family friend; the person chosen should be a man who is close to the bride's family. If the bride has a stepfather it should still be her real father who gives her away if they are on good terms; if not, or if she rarely sees her real father, then the stepfather will probably be the best choice.

Kissing the bride no longer has the significance that it used to have, when it marked the first kiss the couple had exchanged! Nevertheless, some couples still include it, either as part of the ceremony or simply as an impulsive gesture when they are man and wife. If the minister knows the couple well he too may kiss the bride after the marriage, and so may the two fathers, but is extremely bad form for anyone else to kiss her before the groom has had the chance.

Many traditions still have, in some form or another, a symbolic expression of reluctance on the part of the bride. This may take the form of actually running away, or may be something as symbolic as weeping when she leaves home for the last time; in Roman times the bride was symbolically torn from her mother's arms. All these acts seem to date from the times when men went out hunting to capture a suitable bride from a neighbouring tribe or village.

*

In many North African marriages either the bride or the groom or both are painted with patterns of henna. These stain the skin and may last for up to several weeks before they wear off.

Other traditions

Hindu marriages can be very varied; in the laws of Manu, which form the basis of Hindu law, eight separate kinds of marriage are recognised, including marriage by purchase, by fraud, by rape and by consent. The most common form is by gift of the bride to the bridegroom from her father, without other obligations. The most important marriage ceremony consists of the bride and groom joining hands and taking seven steps, although in some traditions the only ceremony is a feast for the two families.

*

Amongst the ancient Kumi tribe the strange ceremony of marriage to a mongo tree exists. First the groom and then the bride is married to the tree and embraces it, and it is only after each partner has done this that they are considered man and wife.

*

The traditional wedding ceremony in Papua required the bride and groom to sit back to back in the middle of a hut, surrounded by the witnesses, while an old man joined their hands and then spat a mouthful of water over them.

*

The Andaman Islands are populated by an aboriginal race that is considered one of the most primitive in the world. Their marriage ceremony, appropriately, is very simple: the bride is brought to an empty hut and sits down; the bridegroom pretends to run away but is brought to the hut also and made to sit on the bride's lap. They are then considered married.

*

In an ancient ceremony from Finland the bride and groom each have to swallow a piece of fungus, used as tinder, that has been set alight.

*

In many Hindu traditions the bride must not speak to or see her groom until the ceremony is completed; in some areas she may even have her eyelids sealed down temporarily with a sticky substance.

*

In ancient Bedouin tribes the girl runs away into the hills when the marriage time is appointed; the groom goes in search of her, and when he finds her they both stay out overnight in the hills. This constitutes the marriage.

*

During traditional Druse weddings in the Middle East the groom would place a very elaborate pointed headdress on the bride's head; this would then be worn by her night and day.

*

In Persia marriage by proxy used to be the general rule; the bride did not need to be present until the actual consummation of the marriage.

The service – The order of service

The order of service

Most couples have an order of service specially printed for the wedding day; this saves the guests from having to riffle through hymnbooks, service books, etc, as all the necessary information is printed on the one sheet. Even if you are marrying in a traditional Church of England ceremony, there are still numerous variations you may want to make, and several decisions you will need to make regarding the details of the order of service.

Choosing the music will need to be done before you have the orders of service printed; you will probably want to put in the titles of the pieces you choose for before and after the ceremony, and during the signing of the register (see pp 148–149 for suggestions!) In addition, you will almost certainly want some hymns; these should be printed out in full in the order of service sheets. Don't feel obliged to have all the verses of your favourite hymns if you don't want them, or if you want to cut down on the time; similarly, don't be afraid to vary the tune if there is one that you prefer to the tune suggested by the hymnbook. Do try and choose at least one hymn that is very well known by all the congregation; if your choice is very obscure you might find yourselves doing a duet!

You will need to sort out the exact order in which the elements of the service occur. Again the Anglican service has a fairly set order, but even this can be varied, for instance by changing when you have the prayers or readings(s), or how many hymns you have before the marriage itself. Most ministers prefer to have the marriage very near the beginning of the service, as most of the other elements – eg prayer, blessing, address – are related to the couple as man and wife.

Generally the minister gives an introduction after the wedding party is assembled at the front of the church, and then a hymn is sung. The marriage usually takes place straight after the first hymn. The minister will list the purposes of marriage, check the intentions of the bride and groom to be a good wife and husband, ask if there are any legal impediments to the marriage, and then supervise the exchange of vows and of rings. He will then declare the couple to be man and wife.

The order of elements in the service may then be arranged according to your own preferences and the minister's. He will offer up some prayers for you as a couple, and if you have a friend or friends whom you would like to pray for you publicly this too can be incorporated. Sometimes the bride and groom will choose to pray for one another publicly, asking God's help as they go on in life as husband and wife.

The minister may give a short address, usually words of advice and well-wishing for the couple as they start married life. There are often one or two readings from the Bible; these may be read by the minister, by friends or relations, or by the couple themselves. Usually one or two more hymns are sung, and the religious part of the service is concluded before the wedding party goes into the vestry, as when they come out they will simply process through the church to the door.

The register is signed by the groom, the bride, the person who performed the wedding and two witnesses. It is best to choose the witnesses beforehand, to save everybody rushing when two are asked for; generally it is the best man and the chief bridesmaid, but the choice could be both mothers, both fathers, or one representative from each family. The time during the signing of the register can be very boring for the wedding guests, so it is customary to have something going on in the church meanwhile, such as somebody singing or the organist playing a particular piece, or perhaps a friend playing a flute or violin solo. Whatever it is, try to print the details in the order of service sheet so that the guests know what is going on and whether they ought to be joining in.

Once you have decided on the details of the service, instruct your printer on what you want on your order of service sheets. These can be printed in the same style as your wedding invitations, although of course they will be more extensive. Print all the information that the guests will need, for instance when they are expected to join in with prayers or responses. Printing the music that the wedding party will enter and leave to will also make sure that the guests stand at the right time!

The service – Checklist/Forward planner

Checklist for order of service

What music will be used before the bride arrives?	What piece of music will be played as the bride enters?
Which hymns do we want sung, and in what order?	
Will there be an address?	Will there be prayers?
What reading or readings do we want?	
Who will do the readings?	
Do we want any participation from other friends or relatives, in the way of prayers, music, blessing, etc?	
What will happen when we are signing the register?	How many orders of service will we need? (Remember you will want one for each guest.)
	How do we want them designed?
What music will be played as we leave the church?	Who will print them?
	When can we collect them?

Use this page to plan out your order of service – hymns, music, marriage ceremony, address, readings, prayers, blessing, signing of the register, etc.

Music

Music

Music is an integral part of a wedding service. It adds to the dignity and special air of the occasion, and also contributes one of the notes of rejoicing and celebration. Also, it provides a chance for the couple to choose one or more pieces of music that are special to them for one reason or another. Most church weddings are accompanied by organ music as that is the most easily available instrument in that setting. Also the organ will be powerful enough to fill the whole church with music, whereas a soloist on another instrument such as an oboe or violin may not be loud enough to cover the bustle of everyone getting to their feet and saying how lovely the bride looks!

---------*---------

Before the service

Ushers, guests and the groom and best man will be at the church well before the bride, so it is best if your organist has a repertoire that will keep him or her occupied for at least 20 minutes before the bride is due. This helps to get people into the wedding mood, and also gives them the chance to listen to some enjoyable, relaxing music while they wait. The music can be of any kind the organist chooses but it is best to keep it fairly sober and classical, unless something like ragtime or old time musichall fits in with the style of the rest of your wedding!

---------*---------

As the bride arrives

The entrance of the bride may be greeted by a fanfare or a trumpet voluntary (depending on the talent you have at your disposal), and then the bride enters, usually to something relatively stately to mark the significance of what is about to happen. Before the (now rather hackneyed) *Wedding March* ('Here comes the bride') was first played in 1850, favourites used to be Handel's *Occasional Overture* or Mendelssohn's music from *A Midsummer Night's Dream*. The Wagner *Wedding March* (actually the *Bridal Chorus* from his opera *Lohengrin*) then swept the board for popularity, although other favourites in Victorian times included Handel's *Processional March* and *March* from *Hercules*, Mendelssohn's *March* from *Athalie*, and Beethoven's *Hallelujah Chorus* from the *Mount of Olives*. More recently, brides have entered to Bach's *Jesu Joy of Man's Desiring* and Verdi's *March* from *Aida*, amongst others.

While the register is being signed

Try to arrange for some music to be played during this time, even if it is merely the organist repeating some of the pieces played before the service. This is the traditional time for friends of the bride and groom to play, or sing, or both, or if a choir has been hired this will be their chief spot. You can either choose the music yourself or leave it to the musicians concerned, depending on the extent of your own musical knowledge.

----------------*----------------

As you leave the church

Something triumphant and joyful is the keynote here; you are announcing to the world that you are married! Again you may have a piece of music that is special to you, but if not there are many suitable classical and modern pieces.

----------------*----------------

Some guidelines

You will need to check very carefully that the music you want is suitable for being played on the organ that is in the church. Some pieces can sound very grand played on a good organ by an excellent musician, but sound extremely weak played on a poor organ by an indifferent organist, in a church with dreadful acoustics. If you are using the church's regular organist he or she will be able to advise you on the best pieces to be played on that particular organ; even if you are importing your own organist, it's worth picking the brains of the regular one who will tell you which kind of music sounds best in that church. You may want to have your own music composed for your wedding, in which case you will need to be sure you have the musicians and the instruments to do it justice. If both organ and organist seem hopeless, all is not lost; a wide variety of tapes are available that can be played on any good PA system, so you can still have good-quality music.

Music – Making the selection

Musical selection

Listed here are some pieces that are suitable for playing at various times during the service.

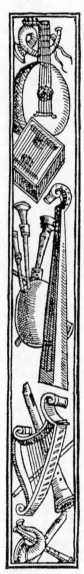

As the bride arrives

Brahms	*Theme* from the *St Anthony Chorale*
Charpentier	*Prelude to a Te Deum*
Clarke	*Prince of Denmark's March*
Guilmant	*March on Lift up your Heads*
Handel	*Hornpipe in D* from the *Water Music*
	Hornpipe in F from the *Water Music*
	March from *Scipio*
	Coro from the *Water Music*
	Minuet No 2 from the *Water Music*
	Arrival of the Queen of Sheba
	March from the *Occasional Oratorio*
Harris	*Wedding Processional*
Hollins	*A Trumpet Minuet*
Parry	*Bridal March*
Purcell	*Trumpet tune*
	Rondeau from *Abdelazar*
Verdi	*Grand March* from *Aida*
Wagner	*Bridal March* from *Lohengrin*
Walton	*March* from *Richard III*
	Crown Imperial

For the entrance or the recessional

Boyce	*Trumpet Voluntary*
Bride	*Allegro Marzialle*
Guilmant	*Allegro* from *Sonata in D minor*
Karg-Elert	*Praise the Lord O My Soul*
Mendelssohn	*Sonata No 3* (first movement)
Stanley	*Trumpet Voluntary* from *Suite in D*
Suttle	*Wedding March*
Wesley	*Choral Song*

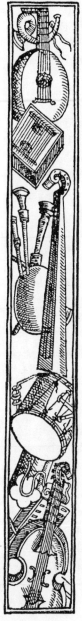

While the register is being signed

Albinoni	*Adagio in G minor*
Bach	*Air* from *Suite in D*
	Sheep may safely graze
	Adagio from *Toccato Adagio and Fugue*
	Jesu, Joy of Man's Desiring
Brahms	*Behold, a rose is blooming*
Handel	*Minuet* from *Berenice*
	Air from the *Water Music*
Macdowell	*To wild rose*
Mendelssohn	*Allegretto* from *Sonata No 4*
Mozart	*Romanze* from *Eine Kleine Nachtmusik*
Schubert	*Ave Maria*
Schumann	*Traumerei*
Vaughan-Williams	*Chorale Prelude on Rhosymedre*
Wesley	*Air* from *Three Pieces*

As the couple leave the church

Dubois	*Toccata in G*
Guilmant	*Grand Choeur in D*
Fletcher	*Festive Toccata*
Karg-Elert	*Now thank we all our God*
Mendelssohn	*Wedding March* from *A Midsummer Night's Dream*
Mulet	*Carrilon-Sortie*
Smart	*Postlude in D*
Vierne	*Carrilon in B flat*
	Final from *Symphony No 1*
Walton	*Crown Imperial*
Whitlock	*Fanfare*
Widor	*Toccata* from *Symphony No 5*

Photographs

Photographs

Your photographs are a very important reminder of your wedding day, not just for you, but for your parents, friends, attendants, etc. It is vital to make sure that you have a good photographer that you can trust. This doesn't necessarily mean having a professional wedding photographer; if you have a friend or relative who is a *very* good photographer and you want to rely on him or her, then that should be fine. Don't, however, rely just on friends' snapshots; these will be nowhere near the high quality that you will want for your special photographs. Another advantage of professional photographers is that their service is probably covered by insurance; certainly you will be eligible for compensation should something go horribly wrong with the film or with the final negatives.

*

Don't rush into the decision of which photographer to have; take your time to make sure that you have the best possible deal. If you have a friend or neighbour in the same town whose wedding photographs are particularly good, ask her which photographer she used. Go round to all the local photographers and ask to see their brochures; some firms specialise in certain types of print, and you may know straight away that a particular firm is not the one you are looking for.

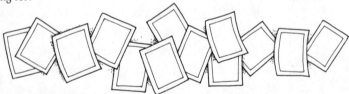

Once you have narrowed the choice slightly, ask to see more examples of the work and also check what kind of package deal the firm offers. Some firms sell a deal that might include, for instance, pictures all through the day, thirty prints from the proofs of your choice, and a free album to keep them in, all for a set sum; other prints ordered by guests will be extra. Other firms might offer simply a higher price for each print you choose, with no extra fee for the actual photography. Still other firms might do particular offers on 'special effect' photographs – prints of the couple with a misty finish, or superimposed on a champagne glass or ribbon bow, or prints in heart–shaped frames.

*

Obviously which deal you choose depends on what your particular requirements and preferences are. If you are having a relatively small wedding and know that you will not want all that many photographs, you may find it more economical to choose one of the firms that simply charges per print. If you are having a very large wedding, and perhaps wanting photographs of all the guests, then you may do better with a firm that charges a flat fee for the day and then a smaller fee per print. Compare the prices stringently, and don't let the firm push you into having a service that you don't want.

Once you have settled on the firm that you feel will be best for your wedding, check that they have a photographer available for the day of your wedding. Make it clear whether you want photographs taken at your parents' home, of the guests before the service, during the service itself, afterwards outside the church, at the reception, and as you leave for your honeymoon. Specify whether you want just formal shots, just informal ones, or a mixture of both. Ask for all these points to be confirmed in writing; this may seem cold-blooded, but it is important to avoid any confusion later on. Double-check that the firm has booked the times correctly, including the time beforehand and the time that the reception is due to finish.

*

One point that it is important to get sorted out very early on in the proceedings is whether or not photographs and video recordings are allowed inside the church. This is the decision of the minister alone, and is not really open to negotiation; it is his church, and you must respect his decision. Some ministers permit photographs as long as no flashes or floodlights are used, others are happy as long as no photographs are taken during the actual marriage itself, while still others will not allow any photographs inside the church. Ask about this before you book your photographer, so that you can brief him or her accordingly.

*

Finally, ask to see examples of the work done by the very photographer who will be covering your wedding, not just publicity shots for the firm in general; any reputable firm should be quite happy to show you these, so that you can assess his or her skill for yourself.

151

Photographs – Checklist/Video checklist

Checklist for wedding photography

Is photography allowed in the church?	How much is the service likely to cost?
If so, are there any restrictions on when the photographs may be taken at different parts of the service?	What formal and informal shots do we want? ☐ Bride at her dressing table ☐ Bride putting on her veil or hat ☐ Bridesmaids getting bride ready ☐ Bride and her parents at the house ☐ Bride and bridesmaids in the garden ☐ Each guest arriving at the church ☐ Best man and groom before the ceremony ☐ Bridesmaids arriving ☐ Bride and her father arriving ☐ Wedding party assembled ☐ Bride going down the aisle ☐ Marriage itself ☐ Leaving the church or registry office
Do we want glossy or matt prints?	☐ Bride and groom together ☐ Couple with best man, bridesmaids and other attendants
Do we want photographs taken of the bride as she is getting ready?	☐ All attendants together
If so, at what time should the photographer arrive?	☐ Couple with both sets of parents ☐ Couple with bride's family ☐ Couple with groom's family
Do we want photographs of the guests arriving?	☐ Oldest and youngest wedding guests ☐ Speeches ☐ Cutting the cake
If so, at what time should the photographer arrive at the church or registry office?	☐ Receiving line at the reception ☐ Leaving for honeymoon
	When will the proofs be ready?
Is there a flat fee for the firm we have chosen, or do they charge by the print?	When do we have to pay the photographer?

Videos

More and more couples these days are having their weddings and receptions recorded on video. This can be done by a professional firm, or it can be done by a sensible amateur; if you are using a friend or relative to provide this service, choose someone who you know takes clear, steady, consistent videos. Once again you may find that the minister will not allow the service itself to be recorded on video, but some may be willing.

High points that you are likely to want to record are the bride getting ready, guests and the wedding party arriving at the ceremony, the ceremony itself (if allowed), signing the register (which may be allowed even if the service itself cannot be recorded), leaving the church, greeting guests at the reception, the speeches and toasts, cutting the cake, and leaving for honeymoon. Once again check and compare costs of professional firms; some offer a professional make-up service as part of their package. Ask to see a sample wedding video to check that it is the quality and approach that you are happy with.

Video checklist

Do we want our wedding recorded on video?	Will the video be allowed inside the church?
Who will do it?	Will it be allowed inside the registry office, or when we are signing the register?
What will it cost?	Can we have the original video copied?
What will the cost include?	If so, how many copies will we want?
	When will we need to pay for the service provided?

Transport

Transport

Transport to and from the service and reception is one of the finishing touches to your wedding. You may have always dreamed of arriving in a white Rolls-Royce, or leaving your reception in a hot air balloon; now is the time to make your dreams come true, provided cash is no problem!

The most conventional way of travelling is to hire sleek black or white wedding cars from a specialised firm; these may be Daimlers, Rolls-Royces, Rovers, Jaguars or other smart and prestigious models. Other firms offer black or white London taxis, vintage cars of various models, and large limousines for large wedding parties! If you find that you cannot afford to hire cars, or all the cars you need for the wedding party, check up among your friends and relations for smart cars that could be beribboned on the day; they don't need to be black or white – in fact scarlet, blue, dark green or silver would look very classy and a bit unusual into the bargain. If money is no object you may want to go for one of the more extreme forms of transport offered by some wedding firms – vintage buses, horse and carriage, pony and trap, etc; but if you choose an open carriage or car, don't forget that it may rain!

You will need transport for the bride's mother to church – she may well be driven there by the rest of the bride's family, or by family friends who can pick her up on the way to church. The formal cars are generally needed for the bride and her father to arrive at the church (this car is then usually used to transport the newly married couple to the reception), and for any bridesmaids (this car may be used to carry the bridesmaids and best man to the reception). Of course, if you have many attendants, you will need still more formal transport.

Once the couple have been taken to the reception venue the hired chauffeur's duties are usually over, although you can retain the car to take you to your first-night destination if you wish. More commonly, you will want to hire or arrange a car to take you on honeymoon from the reception – preferably hidden somewhere close by meanwhile, out of the reach of mischievous hands!

In some North African tribes the bride is swaddled in blankets, put on the back of a female relative, and carried into the courtyard where she is placed in a 'bridal box'. This is a wooden frame draped in a large blanket and placed on the back of a camel or horse.

Transport checklist

How many formal cars will we need?	Will the cars be decorated?
Will we borrow them or hire them?	If so, how?
If hiring, from which firm?	
How long will we need them for?	
How much will it cost?	What time will we need them to collect the various people?
Do they have back-up cars if one should develop a fault?	Do we want any special kind of transport?
Do they have back-up chauffeurs?	
What will the chauffeurs wear?	Do we want any particular colour car?
	What transport will we need to go on honeymoon?
	Where will we get it?
	Where will we hide it?

In Chinese weddings couples often did not actually meet until the wedding ceremony. The bride was conveyed to her future husband's house in a curtained sedan chair decorated in red, the wedding colour of the Chinese.

*

In traditional Greek ceremonies the bridegroom must ride to the bride's house on horseback while the youths of the village try to block his way. If he succeeds in riding through them, they must carry him into the house on their clasped hands.

*

In Hervey Island in the South Seas, if the bride is the eldest daughter she has to walk to her groom's house on a path made by members of her husband's tribe as they lie face down on the ground.

155

The day itself

꧁꧂꧁꧂꧁꧂꧁꧂꧁꧂꧁꧂꧁꧂꧁꧂꧁꧂꧁꧂꧁꧂

The day itself

By the time the big day dawns, everyone should have a very clear idea of what their duties are and when they should perform them. It is a good idea to have a rehearsal for the actual service in the church, so that everyone knows just where they should be standing at what time; the best time to do this is soon before the wedding, so that as many as possible of the actual participants can attend.

* * *

When the bride wakes up in the morning it will still seem as though there are 101 things to do, but if you have been well organised through the preceding weeks the whole procedure will probably run like clockwork! The bride will spend the hour or two before the wedding getting ready for her honeymoon and checking that everything is packed, getting changed into her bridal attire, and having her photograph taken if the photographer has been booked to come to the house.

*

Meanwhile, at the church...the ushers will have arrived 45–60 minutes before the service is due to start so that they are there to greet any early guests, to make sure that they know what their duties are, and to be ready with the orders of service. About 20 minutes before the service the minister will arrive, and so will the groom and best man. The groom and best man will pose for photographs, and the best man will pay the fees on behalf of the groom and make sure that the ushers know what they are doing. If you are having bellringing this will probably take place for about half an hour before the service; inside the church the organist will have arrived about half an hour early and will be playing quietly as the guests begin to arrive.

*

Most guests will arrive about 15 minutes before the service begins. The ushers will give them each an order of service and show them to their appropriate seats. Depending on the size of the church and the size of the wedding, the first one or two pews are reserved for the couple's families, the second one or two for more distant relations, and the pews behind that are for friends. The groom's family and friends traditionally sit on the right, behind the groom, and the bride's family and friends on the left, behind where the bride will stand.

*

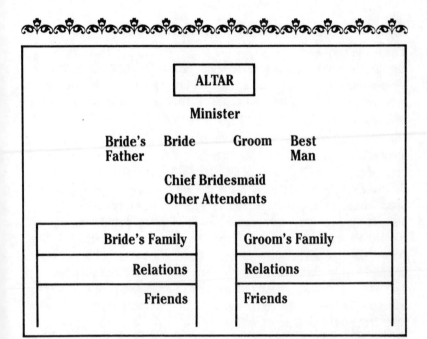

	ALTAR		
	Minister		
Bride's Father	Bride	Groom	Best Man
	Chief Bridesmaid		
	Other Attendants		

Bride's Family	Groom's Family
Relations	Relations
Friends	Friends

About 10 minutes before the ceremony is due to begin the bride's mother arrives; she is personally escorted to her seat by one of the ushers, and sits in the front pew on the left of the church. She must remember to keep a seat spare on her right so that the bride's father can sit down when he has completed his part in the service. The bride's mother should be the last guest to arrive; if there are any latecomers the ushers should slip them into the back seats with the minimum of fuss and attention, so that people are not distracted from the ceremony itself.

*

Also about 10 minutes before the service the bridesmaids arrive. The chief bridesmaid will check that everyone looks smart and that all the junior attendants know what they are doing, and they will all have some photographs taken.

The day itself – The bride arrives

The bride arrives

The bride's arrival will usually be timed perfectly by the chauffeur so that she arrives within one or two minutes of the set time for the wedding. She may have one or two photographs taken with her father and with all the attendants, and then the wedding party will group ready to go down the aisle.

The organist or trumpeter will begin the chosen wedding march, and the groom and best man will rise from their seats at the front of the church and stand at the head of the aisle; the minister will be in position at the front of the church. The bride comes down the aisle on her father's right arm so that she will be standing next to the groom when she reaches the head of the aisle. In some cases she may be preceded by a flower girl scattering petals or confetti. Behind her will come any pages that are actually helping to carry her train. If there are no trainbearers the next person in the procession is the chief bridesmaid, followed by any other bridesmaids and junior attendants such as flower girls and pages. If there are only two bridesmaids they may walk down together, but if they are of very different heights it is better for the taller one to precede the smaller.

The groom and best man turn to greet the bride as she arrives at the front of the church, and the chief bridesmaid takes the bride's bouquet and lifts her veil if she has one. The minister or the best man provides the wedding party with orders of service if they need them; the minister issues a greeting to everyone present, and then a hymn is usually sung as a prelude to the marriage itself.

The minister will give a general introduction to the wedding, and then will ask who is giving the bride to be married. The bride's father may reply or just nod or step forward; he takes the bride's right hand and presents it palm down to the minister. The minister in turn places it in the right hand of the groom. The bride's father's role in the ceremony is now over, and he takes his place in the pew beside the bride's mother.

The minister takes the bride and groom through their wedding vows and charges anyone who knows any reason why they should not be married to declare it. The bride and groom often exchange rings as part of the ceremony. It is the best man's duty to keep the rings safe and to present them to the minister at the appropriate time. The minister may take them on his service book or in his hand; he may bless them, or simply hand them to the bride and groom at the appropriate moment. The groom places the bride's ring on her wedding finger and says the words telling her what the ring symbolises; if he too is having a ring the bride does the same for him. The minister will then declare that having met all the legal requirements and having made a public declaration of their intention to marry, the couple are now man and wife. He will then pray for the couple, and may give a short address.

The minister leads the way to the vestry for the signing of the register, followed by the bride on the groom's left arm. They in turn are followed by the bride's mother on the arm of the groom's father, and then the groom's mother on the arm of the bride's father. After them come the bridesmaid and the best man, followed by any other adult attendants; small attendants may be provided with places at the front of the church if desired. In the vestry the register is signed by the person performing the marriage, the groom, the bride (using her maiden name) and the two chosen witnesses.

The day itself – Leaving the church

Leaving the church

After the signing of the register, the wedding party proceeds down the aisle and out of the church. The bride and groom go first, attended by any small bridesmaids or pages needed to carry the bride's train. After the couple come the chief bridesmaid and the best man, and any junior bridesmaids, and these are followed by the bride's mother accompanied by the groom's father, then the groom's mother accompanied by the bride's father.

As the couple leave the church, they are often scattered with confetti – small brightly-coloured pieces of tissue paper in pretty shapes or shaped like rose petals. Confetti is the Italian word for confectionery, or sweets, which is what was formerly used, symbolising wishes that the marriage would be attended by lots of sweet experiences. In this country real flowers were often used, or their petals, until the advent of paper confetti. These days, in our technological era, the circles made by punching holes in computer paper are often used! It is important to ask whether confetti is allowed outside or near the church – some ministers, understandably, object to the amount of clearing up that it necessitates.

Rice is also a traditional form of confetti in this country – and grain of some sort or another is used in many countries – because of its symbolism with fertility. Sometimes the grain is in the form of small cakes, which in fact are the origin of our own wedding cakes. The bride used to be showered with them, but now she can keep the cake intact for her guests to share in! Fruit and nuts and raisins are also used as confetti in some cultures, again symbolising the wish that the marriage should be rich and fruitful.

Outside the church the wedding party may emerge under a guard of honour of ceremonial swords, a canopy of ribbons, or to a reception in keeping with their hobbies or interests – for instance a football team suitably dressed, or a party of schoolchildren if one of the couple is a teacher. Bells are often rung as the couple leaves, traditionally a way of letting the whole town know that the wedding has taken place.

In Roman times, grooms threw nuts at their attendants as the marriage ceremony finished.

In Elizabethan times the congregation could grab for favours from the bride – these could be anything from ribbons and buttons to gloves, girdles, purses and garters.

In some rural areas of Britain the path in front of the newly married couple would be strewn with symbols of the groom's trade, for instance cloth for a weaver or tailor, woodshavings for a carpenter, scraps of iron or tools for a blacksmith.

In Italy bonbons, sugared almonds and tiny cakes can be scattered over the bride and groom; the cakes may be made in the shapes of hearts, flowers and good luck symbols.

In Cleveland attendants used to fire a gun charged with feathers over the newly-married couple, as a wish that nothing harder would fall on them throughout their marriage.

In Barmby Moor during the last century the minister had to leave the church very quickly after he had performed a marriage ceremony, as it was traditional for the congregation to shower him with hassocks and hymnbooks.

At traditional Czechoslovakian weddings the bride and groom would emerge from the church under a canopy of ribbons stretched out by a party of attendants dressed in national costume.

In Moravia the path taken by the couple as they left the wedding ceremony would be decorated in elaborate patterns of chalk.

What type

※※※※※※※※※※※※※※※※※※※※※※※※※※※※※※※※※※※

Reception

Once you have decided on the venue, there are numerous other details to be
checked regarding your reception. Remember that you and your guests will
almost certainly be at the reception far longer than you are at the service, so it
is important to get everything as right as possible!

The seating is an important consideration. Are you going to have a sit-down
meal? If so, is there somewhere where the guests can relax more informally
and mingle more freely, both before and after the meal? Are the chairs
comfortable? Are there high-chairs and cushions available for small children?
If you are having a buffet you will need to decide whether you still want tables
and chairs set up for all the guests, or whether the guests will be expected to
stand. You will only be able to expect them to stand all the time if it is a very
short, informal buffet, and even then you will need to provide seats for elderly
or infirm guests.

If you are having lots of children among your guests make sure that the
facilities are adequate for them. Ideally there should be somewhere where
they can play if they get bored, which is especially likely with a long, formal
reception. Also you will need to bear them in mind when you are planning the
eating arrangements – is it the kind of food that children are likely to enjoy,
and if not, do you want to provide a separate menu for the children? Are there
suitable implements around for them to eat with? Are there lots of soft
drinks?

The catering is a vital consideration in any reception. If you hire an hotel or
restaurant you can often choose to have their caterers preparing and serving
the food, and of course doing the clearing up afterwards. Alternatively, you
may want to use outside caterers if you are having the reception in a hall,
marquee, hotel, restaurant or home. When choosing your caterer go by
recommendation if you can; all firms will tell you that they provide a good
service, but there is nothing to beat the recommendation of someone who has
been extremely pleased with their services.

You may decide that you want to do the catering yourself, or with the help of
friends or relatives. Never underestimate the amount of time and preparation
all this will take; especially if it is a formal reception the work will be
phenomenal. Only do this if you genuinely enjoy catering for large numbers
and if you have adequate facilities and adequate back-up in terms of
washer-uppers, servers, etc. It is perfectly possible for a team of

✳✳✳✳✳✳✳✳ ✳✳✳✳✳✳✳✳✳✳✳✳✳ ✳✳✳✳✳✳✳✳✳✳✳✳

well-organised friends and relations to serve up a delicious meal without too much trouble on the day as long as the plans have been carefully laid. Some people will choose to serve a full meal such as casseroles, pies, salad, etc, plus desserts; others may prefer to prepare a buffet. Choose food that can be prepared in advance and frozen; if you have access to a caterer's freezer or fridge this will be very useful.

Don't forget all the accessories, such as cutlery, crockery, glassware, tablecloths and napkins, bottle openers, cake stand and knife, etc. Once again, if you use professional caterers they should provide all these extras (although it is worth checking in detail), but if you or friends are doing the catering you will need to provide them yourselves. Look in your telephone directory for firms that specialise in hiring out equipment, and check on deliveries, collections, insurance and breakages. You may choose to order some of the specially printed wedding tableclothes and paper napkins – and even plates. These are generally of very low quality and often in extremely bad taste. You may well do better to buy from one of the very attractive printed ranges of disposable accessories available from large stationery stores; these are prettier, much better quality, and their higher price can be offset by the money you save by not having the wedding goods personalised.

Timing is an important question; even when you have worked out what time you want the reception to begin and end you still have to work out what time you want the meal served, and whether you can have access to the reception venue earlier in the day to check that everything is OK, to put the cake in position, etc. Each venue will vary on these arrangements, so make sure that both parties are sure what the arrangements are; ask for them to be put in writing so that there is no dispute.

What type – Alternative receptions

Doing things differently
If you are having a small wedding, or alternatively if you are having a very large one and money is no object, you may want to do something a little bit different for your reception. On pages 42–43 we've mentioned some radical ideas for alternative kinds of wedding reception, but you might want to go for a half-way stage.

For instance, you might want to have your wedding reception on a boat. This is a relatively common form of reception for those who live near water, and a look in your telephone directory will give you the contacts with people and firms who have suitable boats for hire. Once again caterers may be provided or you may need to provide your own; entertainment may be included in the hire. A boat is a rather exotic setting that is both out of a building and yet also under cover, which is a good idea in case the weather is unreliable.

Alternatively, you may want to have a less formal type of reception in your home or a hall. In America more unusual forms of reception are quite customary – for instance, a cocktail party, a cheese and wine party, or a teatime reception with snacks and cakes rather than a full meal. Or you could choose a party that combines a relatively traditional reception with something a bit different – for instance, if you are using a large hall you could clear some of it for country dancing, ballroom dancing or a disco. If there are to be lots of children you could invite a clown or magician to entertain them. Or you (or the best man!) could lay on a slide show of photographs and films of you both growing up and significant stages in your courtship!

Music is another way of making your wedding reception that little bit different. Most of the wedding magazines, and most local papers, offer the services of all kinds of musicians such as harpists, steel bands, string quartets, singers, barbershop singers, jazz musicians, pianists, etc. And, of course, there are always disc jockeys available with discos, light shows, etc; your guests may be able to stay on for a party after you have left on honeymoon.

Checklist for wedding reception

How many people will be invited to the reception?	Who will provide the table linen?
Will it be formal or informal?	When will the cake be delivered to the reception venue?
Do we want a sit-down meal, buffet or something else?	Are there adequate bar facilities?
	Are there adequate toilet/cloakroom facilities?
What venue will be best?	What are the insurance arrangements?
Who will be doing the catering?	Are there adequate car parking facilities?
Is there any hire charge for the venue?	Are there any restrictions on alcohol consumption?
If so, when does it have to be paid?	Are there any restrictions on smoking?
Are there facilities for tea and coffee?	Is there room for the wedding cars to draw up outside?
Are the chairs comfortable?	Is there a separate table for the cake, etc?
Is the decor attractive?	Do we need a Master of Ceremonies?
Will we need flowers to decorate the room?	If so, who will do the job?
If so, are they provided?	Are there attractive places for photographs to be taken?
Is there somewhere for the children to play?	Who will deal with our enquiries?
Will we be able to go outside if the weather is good?	
Who will provide crockery, cutlery and glasses?	What is his or her telephone number?
	Will he or she be on hand on the day?

Where

The reception

Choosing the right time, place and atmosphere for your wedding reception will help to ensure that your wedding celebrations are conducted to your entire satisfaction! Put a lot of thought into the details of your reception; it will not be wasted time, and will help to guarantee that on the day everything runs smoothly and everyone has a good time.

What kind of a reception do you want? Conventional receptions come in many forms: formal, sit-down meals, hot or cold buffets, parties at home or in a hall or marquee, evening parties for friends and relations. Your style of reception should echo the style of your wedding ; for instance, if you are having a very formal, very large church wedding with all the trimmings then a formal sit-down reception in an hotel or restaurant would be appropriate. On the other hand, if you are having a very small, quiet registry office wedding you may want to have a small buffet reception at your mother's home.

Decide on the kind of reception you want, and then decide on an appropriate venue. Ideally the reception should be close to the church or registry office, or at least within an easy car journey; in any case it is often best to issue guests with a map to prevent anyone from getting lost! As soon as you know the venue of your wedding service you can look for a suitable place nearby to hold the reception. Many people hire the functions room of an hotel or restaurant; these can often be hired with or without the establishment's own catering staff, but it is wise to check this at the time. Hotels and restaurants have the advantages that their rooms are generally attractive and spacious, they are (or should be) well decorated, they generally have ample parking space, and will be used to hosting this kind of venture and so will be able to help it go smoothly.

If there is no suitable hotel or restaurant nearby, or if you want to save money or have a less formal reception, you could hire or borrow a hall such as the church's own hall, a room in a sports club or civic building, etc. Halls can vary from the very shabby and stark to the very pleasant, so always ask to see the hall if this is what you choose to do. Also you will have to bear in mind the catering arrangements; does the hall have a kitchen nearby? What are the arrangements for making tea and coffee? Where will drinks be served? Are there any restrictions on serving alcohol? Are there any restrictions on dancing, if you want to include this as part of the celebrations?

✷✸✷✸✷✸✷✸✷✸✷✸✷✸✷✸✷✸✷✸ ✷✸✷✸✷✸✷✸✷✸✷✸✷✸✷✸✷✸✷✸

You may have a burning desire to have your wedding reception at home. This can be a lovely way for a bride's mother to say goodbye to her daughter from the home where she was brought up – but it can also be an easy way of having a nervous breakdown, especially when all the necessary arrangements for the reception are combined with all the last-minute details before a wedding. It is possible, of course, to use your home but have outside caterers to do all the preparation, clearing up and serving, which can be a good compromise.

Marquees are popular for wedding receptions for many reasons; they can be erected in the grounds of a house, hotel or other building without intruding on what is going on inside, and they form a pretty and elegant background for the celebrations. Marquees can be hired on their own from specialist firms, or they can be ordered as part of an entire wedding package from some caterers. If you are thinking of having a marquee, ask if you can see photographs of how it will look erected, whether it will damage the ground that it stands on, what the decoration will be like inside, whether it will stand up to heavy rain, etc; also, think of the practicalities of where it will stand – is there a car park nearby? How far do the guests have to walk to a cloakroom? Will they have to walk through mud if it rains?

If you are having difficulty in selecting a venue, ask yourself some basic questions about each possibility. Are they big enough? Are they attractive? Are the toilet, car park, bar, kitchen, seating facilities good enough? Are the people helpful? Are there any restrictions on time? What are the insurance arrangements? These should help you to narrow down your choices to the ideal venue for your reception.

Food

Food

Good food makes for a good reception, and if you provide your guests with something tasty as part of a special celebration they will certainly remember the day with affection! The food doesn't have to be exotic and super-extravagant; a selection of well-chosen dishes with differing tastes and textures, served attractively, will give just the right impression however much – or little – you can afford to spend on the menu.

If you are using a caterer the firm will supply you with different menus to choose from, whether you are having a sit-down meal or a buffet. The prices will vary from around £10 per head for a basic, simple, finger buffet to £30 a head or more if you are having an exclusive sit-down menu using expensive ingredients. Certainly you will be able to find a menu that will be tasty and attractive to fit into your set budget. It is worth comparing the services and menus offered by caterers; don't be afraid to ask for sample menus from many firms so that you can check their value for money.

Sit-down meals need to be chosen particularly carefully, as generally everyone will be required to have the same food; this means that you will need to choose relatively 'safe' dishes that everyone will like. So dishes such as liver, seafood, curry, etc, may be best avoided, unless you know that most of your friends and relations like unusual foods. Most people go for a basic ingredient such as chicken, turkey or beef for the main course; if these are to be roasted, make sure that the quality of the roast and the vegetables is high so that people don't feel that they are simply sitting down for a school dinner. For something a little bit different you could arrange for a 'safe' ingredient to be cooked in a slightly unusual way, for instance, chicken casseroled with white wine and cream, beef cooked en croûte, chicken portions baked with bacon and mushrooms, etc. For starters and dessert again it is best to stick to something relatively safe, although a sit-down meal does at least give the opportunity to serve dishes that can't be eaten at a buffet, for instance soups, hot desserts, etc.

Buffets can be either finger buffets, where everything can be eaten with the fingers so that no cutlery is needed, or fork buffets. If the guests are going to be standing all the time it is best to serve a finger buffet; it can be very trying juggling a glass, napkin, plate and fork while standing – and trying to eat as well! You will also need to decide whether you are going to have any hot dishes; this is easier if you are using facilities of an hotel or restaurant which have their own good, large kitchens for heating food.

Whichever type of meal you are having, remember to check whether any of your guests are vegetarian or have other diets such as gluten-free, low salt, kosher, etc. If you are having a buffet most people will be able to select a satisfactory meal for themselves whatever their requirements, but for a sit-down meal you may need to have special portions of alternative foods available. Remember, too, that not all vegetarians eat fish or eggs, so these might not be suitable substitutions.

If you are doing the catering yourself, two main considerations will occupy your thoughts; the first is how much to make of all the dishes, and the second is how to store them. If you are arranging a sit-down meal it is fairly easy to judge the portions; simply estimate the average meal for one person (eg half an avocado, 28g (1oz) prawns, tbsp seafood dressing, 2 slices turkey, 1 large baked potato, 113g (4oz) salad, 1 slice gâteau) and then multiply by the number of guests. If you are doing a buffet, things are a little more complicated. Caterers generally work on the assumption of 15–20 'bits' per person – a bit being one item such as a stuffed hard-boiled egg, a helping of salad, a canape, a vol-au-vent, etc. If the items you are preparing are large, such as individual strawberry tarts or large vol-au-vents, then keep the numbers down to 10–15 items per person. Then arrange your menus so that in total they produce the required number of servings for the expected number of guests. Do everything you can in advance, for instance, preparing whole dishes and freezing them, baking cakes and storing them in airtight tins. On the day, enlist the help of people who will not be at the service to lay out the food, keeping it covered until the last minute so that it stays fresh and attractive.

Food – Ideas for the menu

Menu ideas for a sit-down meal
Typical menu for an economical, fairly safe three-course meal:
Prawn cocktail or melon; roast chicken with roast potatoes, carrots and peas;
fruit flan and cream or chocolate gâteau.
Sample menu for a more exotic three-course meal:
Chilled vichyssoise or gazpacho; sole stuffed with crab and baked in white
wine, served with piped creamed potatoes and broccoli mornay; fresh fruit
pavlova or melon in kirsch.

Ideas for starters
Melon, avocado vinaigrette or with prawns, florida cocktail, prawn cocktail,
grapefruit, consommé, lobster soup with cream, green pea soup, minestrone,
eggs mayonnaise, pâté and toast, smoked mackerel fillets, seafood
vol-au-vents, smoked salmon, corn on the cob, tomato soup, deep-fried
mushrooms, French onion soup.

Ideas for main courses
Baked gammon with parsley sauce, cold turkey, beef or chicken salad,
tournedos Rossini, beef en croûte, mild chicken curry with pilau, chicken
baked with tomatoes and onions, lamb cutlets and minted potatoes, pork
steaks baked with apple rings, turkey goulash, steak and kidney pie, chicken
and asparagus pie, turkey and bacon casserole with cream, duck with orange
or cherry sauce, lobster salad.

Ideas for desserts
Poire belle Hélène, peach melba, black forest gâteau, chocolate mousse,
fresh fruit salad, profiteroles, pineapple or strawberry pavlova, fruit sorbets,
raspberry or apricot mousse, black cherry or raspberry cheesecake, syllabub,
lemon meringue pie, apple pie with cinnamon, mincemeat tart, baked apples
with raisins and cream, peaches in brandy, ice cream with hot fudge or
chocolate sauce, crème caramelle.

---

*For the wedding of a farmer's daughter in Pomerania in 1907 the list of
ingredients was: 32cwt flour, 4 pigs, 2 calves, 3 sheep, 32 geese, 18cwt fish, 54
casks of beer, 500 bottles of wine, 300 litres of brandy.*

*In Sussex brides traditionally had a pie containing a whole hen stuffed with
hard-boiled eggs – this was supposed to be symbolic of fertility.*

Menu ideas for buffets

Dishes for a fairly conventional buffet	Dishes for a more unusual buffet
Sausage rolls	Salmon quiche
Stuffed hard-boiled eggs	Cheese and herb straws
Scotch eggs	Tomato and aspic salad
Pâtés	Salad niçoise
Egg and cress sandwiches	Potato salad with ham and peas
Ham sandwiches	Mushroom salad
Cucumber and cream cheese rolls	Chicken and apple salad
Salmon sandwiches	Waldorf salad
Cheese and onion dip	Curried prawn vol-au-vents
Prawn coleslaw dip	Crab or clam dip
Plain coleslaw	Salmon mousse
Celery, carrot sticks, cauliflower pieces and pepper slices to use in dips	Vegetables for dips
	Pinwheel sandwiches
	Double-layer sandwiches
Rice salad	Cream cheese and walnut sandwiches
Tomato and onion salad	Egg and anchovy sandwiches
Lettuce and cucumber salad	Smoked salmon sandwiches
Chicken drumsticks	Asparagus rolled in brown bread
Turkey nuggets	Avocado and prawn salad
Potato salad	Prunes rolled in bacon
Chicken and mushroom vol-au-vents	Pork and apple meatballs
Ritz biscuits	Cheese and sausagemeat meatballs
Cheddar and Cheshire and Edam cheeses	Salmon steaks
Crisps in several flavours	Rolls of salami filled with cream cheese
Twiglets	Duck pâté
Mayonnaise	Liver and bacon pâté
Fruit salad	Mayonnaise with fresh herbs
Profiteroles	Thousand island dressing
Fruit mousses	Lemon cheesecake
Chocolate mousse	Strawberry and almond tarts
Strawberries	Fresh pineapple slices
	Peaches in kirsch
	Ginger mousse
	Coffee gâteau

Food – Checklists

Checklist for doing it yourself

Who will do most of the cooking?	Who will help out on the day?
Who will help out?	
	Who will serve the food?
Where can we store food before the day?	
	Who will do the clearing up?
What is the cooking schedule?	
	What will we do with leftovers?
	Where will we get table linen?
	Where will we get glasses?
	Where will we get crockery and cutlery?
Can all the food be prepared in advance?	
	How much will it all cost?

Checklist for catering firm

Who will be doing the catering?	When do they plan to leave?
	Will any of the food be hot?
How many people will be serving?	Is tea and coffee included?
Do they provide all the crockery, etc?	Will they cut and serve the cake?
Do they provide table linen?	What will happen to any leftovers?
Do they provide glasses?	Will the servers be in uniform?
Does the cost include drinks?	Do their waiting staff seem pleasant and helpful?
Does the cost include VAT?	Are all the arrangements in writing?
Does the cost include insurance?	How much is it going to cost?
When will they arrive at the venue?	

Menu

Use this space to plan the menu you will be having.

Drinks

Drinks

Once you have decided what you are going to eat at your reception, you will need to decide what you are going to have to drink. Choose the drinks to fit in to the general style and formality of the occasion, just as the food should.

***

Before the meal

If possible, arrange for the guests to have access to a drink of some sort as soon as they arrive at the official part of the reception – that is, as soon as they have deposited their coats, tidied up, and gone past the receiving line if there is one. If it is a very large, formal reception, where guests may be waiting around for quite some time before the receiving line starts, you can arrange for them to be served a first drink in a nearby lounge or attractive hallway. Traditionally, sherry is the best drink to offer at this time; you could arrange for a selection of medium or dry so that the guests have some degree of choice. Alternatively you could offer red or white wine, or an alcoholic or non-alcoholic fruit cup. If you are holding the reception in premises where there is a bar, you can arrange for the barman to serve the guests with the drink of their choice as they arrive. At this stage, as at every other stage of the reception, make sure that there are also plenty of non-alcoholic drinks available for children and for adults who prefer soft drinks.

With the meal

If you have arranged a sit-down meal with a set menu, it will be easy to choose a suitable wine or wines to go with it. If you are having very exotic food, you will probably want to arrange a selection of different wines to complement the different courses. If you are having a buffet, the easiest way to deal with the drinks is to have a plentiful supply of both red and white wine and also suitable non-alcoholic drinks; this way the guests can choose what they prefer. Even if the food is a serve-yourself buffet it is generally best to have one or two people (or more, depending on the size of the reception) officially in charge of topping up the glasses.

For the toasts

Champagne is the traditional drink with which to toast the good health of the bride and groom, but if you are running on a fairly tight budget you may want to go for one of the less expensive alternatives, such as Asti Spumante or an ordinary sparkling white or rosé wine. Even if you choose champagne you do not have to pay a fortune for the very best; many of the reputable chainstores market their own champagne at very reasonable prices. If you have been drinking white wine with the meal, there is nothing wrong in toasting the couple in the same wine, but if you have been serving red it would be more appropriate to serve a different wine for the toasts.

After the meal
After the meal you have numerous options for serving drinks; your choice will depend again on the tone, style and budget of the reception. After a large, very formal meal you may want to serve a dessert wine, or brandy, port or liqueurs. You may just wish to serve tea and coffee. Or, if the reception venue has a bar, you could encourage guests to buy any further drinks they want, or you could pay for, say, the first £80 and then guests could buy their own when that kitty has been used up.

Obtaining the drinks
If you are holding the reception at an hotel, restaurant or club, you may find that they insist on supplying the drinks themselves. Others may allow you to import your own drink but charge a corkage for serving it. If you are arranging the drink yourselves, make sure that you deal with a firm that will provide them on sale or return; this way it doesn't matter if you overestimate the amount needed. If the hotel or restaurant is providing the drinks, check that they will charge only for those actually consumed and not a blanket charge.

Checklist for drinks

What will we drink before the meal?
What will we drink with the meal?
What will we use for the toasts?
What arrangements will we make for drinks afterwards?

The cake

The cake
Wedding cakes are a very ancient tradition in many cultures. The Romans ate a 'cake' baked from wheat flour, salt and water as the marriage contract was performed, and tribes such as the Iroquois Indians and the Fiji Islanders have long traditions of the bride offering a cake to her new husband. In this country the Roman type of cake gave way to a spiced bread or biscuit, and by Tudor times sugar, eggs and fruit were added to make a mixture more similar to the rich fruit cake we know today.

***

The traditions of the cake
Originally the custom was to bake many small cakes and to throw them at the bride after the ceremony, or to shower her with them as she entered her new home; in some countries the bride's attendants threw the cakes to the witnesses to the marriage. After the Restoration the fashion of covering a pile of small cakes with marzipan and sugar was introduced from France; the whole edifice could then be broken over the bride's head at an appropriate moment and all the little cakes would shower out. Gradually the pile of small cakes became one large cake that formed the centrepiece of the wedding feast.

Your cake
Your wedding cake will be the focal point of your reception, even if you are only having a casual buffet, and you will probably want to make sure that your own version of this traditional item is a very special reminder of a very special day. You will need to think of the size of cake that you want, its decoration and shape, whether you want more than one tier, and whether you want to incorporate any special features such as real flowers, ribbons, a message or initials, etc.

Who will make it?
Do you want to make your cake yourself, or will it be made by a friend, a relative, a bakery chain, or a cake specialist? Sometimes wedding caterers or hotels that provide wedding receptions will quote for the cost of a cake as well. The traditional recipe is a rich fruit cake but you don't need to keep to this if you don't want to; American tradition is to have a plain white cake under attractive frosting, and some brides in this country choose a plain sponge or a chocolate cake. You could be completely different and have a cherry cake, orange cake, lemon cake or any other recipe to make your cake unusual – and

less filling! If your cake is to be made by a firm of bakers or caterers, ask to taste a sample first to make sure that it is of good quality.

How big?

The size of your cake will depend on the number that you want to feed with it. This will take into account the guests at your reception, any extra pieces that you will want to save for friends, relations, etc, who couldn't come to the wedding, and any pieces you may want for other people such as friends at work or at a social club. Some couples save the top tier of their cake for their first wedding anniversary, the christening of their first child, or their housewarming in their new home – if you want to do this you will have to add the size of the top tier to the amount of cake you need for consumption on the day. Professional caterers work to standard portions; you could work on the principle that a piece of cake 13×6.5cm (2in $\times$ 1in) $\times$ the height of the cake will be ample for each serving. Work this out for a square cake, then convert it to the equivalent if you are having a cake of a different shape. Remember that the cake will be larger once it is covered with marzipan and icing.

Checklist for your wedding cake

Who is going to make the cake?	How big does the cake need to be?
Who is going to ice the cake?	What shape is the cake going to be?
How much is it going to cost?	What recipe do we want?
How early do I need to order the cake?	
How many guests will need a piece at the wedding?	Will it have tiers – if so, how many?
How many people will be unable to come, and will need to be sent a piece?	Do we want any special decoration or features?
Do we want to have any extra pieces for friends, workmates, etc?	
Do we want an extra tier to save?	When will we need to collect the cake?

The cake – Recipes for fruit cake

✳✳✳✳✳✳✳✳✳✳✳✳✳✳✳✳✳✳✳✳✳✳✳✳✳✳✳✳✳✳✳✳✳

Making your own cake

Many people want to make their own wedding cake – not just for economy's sake, but because home made cake is tastier and you have the pride of achievement as well! Here are two recipes for fruit cake. One is very rich and one is slightly lighter, but either will make an excellent wedding cake.

Rich fruit cake

The instruction outside the brackets is for a 6 in round or 5 in square tin.
The first instruction inside the brackets is for an 8 in round or 7 in square tin.
The second instruction inside the brackets is for an 11 in round or 10 in square tin.

Metric	Imperial
170 (340, 680)g plain flour	6 (12, 24) oz plain flour
¼ (½, 2) level tsp mixed spice	¼ (½, 2) level tsp mixed spice
½ (½, 2) level tsp cinnamon	½ (½, 2) level tsp cinnamon
Pinch (large pinch, ½ tsp) salt	Pinch (large pinch, ½ tsp) salt
142 (283, 595)g butter	5 (10, 21)oz butter
142 (283, 595)g sugar	5 (10, 21)oz sugar
Small amount grated lemon zest	Small amount grated lemon zest
3 (5, 11) size 4 eggs, beaten	3 (5, 11) size 4 eggs, beaten
½ (1, 2) tbsp treacle	½ (1, 2) tbsp treacle
1 (2, 3) tbsp brandy	1 (2, 3) tbsp brandy
227 (454, 1134)g currants	8 (16, 40)oz currants
113 (198, 397)g raisins	4 (7, 14)oz raisins
113 (198, 397)g sultanas	4 (7, 14)oz sultanas
57 (142, 283)g glace cherries	2 (5, 10)oz glace cherries
28 (85, 198)g chopped mixed peel	1 (3, 7)oz chopped mixed peel
28 (85, 198)g almonds, blanched and flaked	1 (3, 7)oz almonds, blanched and flaked

1 Pre-heat the oven to a temperature of Gas mark 2/300°F/150°C.
2 Grease and double line the cake tin.
3 Prepare fruit, nuts, and mixed peel; mix them together in a large bowl.
4 Sift flour, salt and spices together into a separate bowl.
5 Cream butter, sugar and lemon zest together until pale and fluffy.

6 Add eggs to creamed mixture a little at a time, beating well after each addition.

7 Fold flour into mixture a little at a time using a metal spoon.

8 Fold brandy and treacle into mixture.

9 Fold fruit and nuts into mixture.

10 Put mixture into prepared tin and bake at Gas mark 2/300°F/150°C for approximately 2½–3 (3½, 7) hours. Cover with greaseproof paper after 1½–2 hours to prevent top over-browning.

11 Cool in tin overnight. Turn out, wrap in double thickness of greaseproof paper, store in airtight tin.

Lighter fruit cake

This recipe is adaptable for any size or shape of cake tin. The quantities given here are for a cake tin of 1 pint capacity. Check the capacity of your chosen tin by filling it with water, and then multiply up the quantities in the recipe as required.

Metric	Imperial
113g plain flour	4 oz plain flour
½ level tsp mixed spice	½ level tsp mixed spice
Pinch salt	Pinch salt
85g butter	3 oz butter
85g soft brown sugar	3 oz soft brown sugar
1 size 2 egg, beaten	1 size 2 egg, beaten
142g currants	5 oz currants
57g sultanas	2 oz sultanas
57g raisins	2 oz raisins
28g glace cherries, chopped	1 oz glace cherries, chopped
28g chopped mixed peel	1 oz chopped mixed peel

Pre-heat the oven to a temperature of Gas mark 2/300°F/150°C. Grease and line the cake tin. Prepare the fruit and the mixed peel and mix them together in a bowl. Sift the flour, salt and mixed spice together into a separate bowl. Cream the butter and sugar until pale and fluffy, then beat in the egg. Fold in the flour using a metal spoon, then fold in the fruit and peel. Place in the prepared tin and bake at Gas mark 2/300°F/150°C until a fine skewer inserted into the centre of the cake comes out clean. Cool in the tin, then store wrapped in greaseproof paper in an airtight tin.

The cake – Shapes and styles

Shapes and styles

There are many different shapes in which your wedding cake can be made. The easiest shapes of all, of course, are square and round; these are also easiest to decorate as they are regular shapes. If you are just having a small wedding celebration you could simply have a single round, square or heart-shaped cake; if you want something more elaborate you might choose two or more tiers, spaced on top of one another by decorative columns (round for round cakes, square for square ones). American brides often place the tiers one on top of the other without pillars so that the different layers can be iced as one cake.

If you want to be more unusual you could go for one of the more elaborate designs – interlocking hearts or rings, a cake iced like a basket of flowers or a box of chocolates, a cake in the shape of a flower or a butterfly, or two cakes made up in the shape of your initials. Cake tins can be bought or hired for all these shapes and many others such as hexagons and octagons, stars, clover leaves and horseshoes.

1 Simple round cake
2 Interlocking heart cake
3 Cake made in the shape of a basket of flowers
4 Two-tiered cake
5 Tiered cake in American style
6 Three-tiered cake

Traditionally, the origin of the tiered wedding cake is attributed to a pastrycook on Ludgate Hill in London. He used to make cakes for the many illegal marriages that took place near the Fleet prison, and apparently decided to copy Sir Christopher Wren's design for the spire of St Bride's Church.

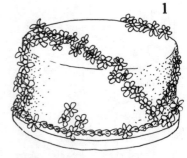

1

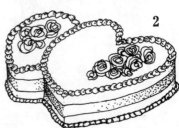

2

3

4

5

6

The cake – Decorating/Colour/At the reception

✳✳✳✳✳✳✳✳✳✳✳✳✳✳✳✳✳✳✳✳✳✳✳✳✳✳✳✳✳✳

Decorating the cake

The decorations you choose for your cake are the main features that will make it uniquely yours. Generally royal icing is used for wedding cakes as it is harder and easier to pipe into fancy shapes, but the relatively recent advent of malleable fondant icing has meant that very attractive finishes can be obtained much more easily. If you are icing your cake yourself look through some of the specialist books to see the many effects that can be used to good advantage on your cake; if you are using a professional ask to see a portfolio of work so that you can choose your own combination of decorations.

Colour schemes

Most wedding cakes are iced in white, but there is no reason why you have to keep to this tradition. The cake offers an ideal opportunity to pick up the colour scheme of the rest of your wedding party – the colours of the flowers, the bridesmaids' dresses, the ribbons in your hair, etc. You may choose to have a Wedgewood effect of white decorations on a pale blue or green icing, or you could have the whole cake iced in a pale shade of yellow, orange, pink, green or blue. Iced flowers and trelliswork can be done in white or in coloured icing, and ribbons and real flowers can be incorporated into the design to make your cake really special. To personalise the cake you could have your initials or names or the date included in the decoration.

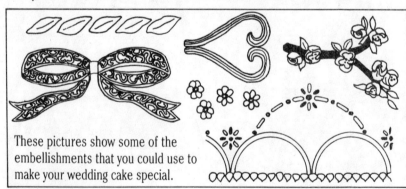

These pictures show some of the embellishments that you could use to make your wedding cake special.

At Jewish weddings the tradition is to cut the cake when dessert is served. The bride cuts the cake with a knife decorated with flowers and ribbons, and then feeds one or two mouthfuls to the groom.

*

At military weddings the cake may be cut with a ceremonial sword instead of a knife.

At the reception

The cake will generally form the focal point of your reception, and the tradition is to place it in the centre of the top table at a sit-down reception, or in the centre of the plates of food at a buffet. However, you might find it more convenient to have a special table set aside for the cake, so that your guests will be able to admire it at their leisure. At some receptions the bride and bridesmaids place their bouquets around the cake; at others the cake is already decorated with flowers – real or imitation – to match the bouquets.

Cutting the cake

This ceremony is usually the last formal part of the reception, although some couples choose to do it before the speeches and toasts so that the cake can be cut up while these are taking place. If the icing is to be very hard, it is sensible to make a cut in the cake before it is iced and to mark its position covertly when the icing is on; this will prevent bride and groom from struggling with a sharp knife in an unseemly way! The bride and groom usually cut the cake together, with the groom's hand covering the bride's. The cake is then removed to be cut up into small pieces and distributed to the guests. If you are saving one of the tiers, arrange for it to be wrapped in greaseproof paper and stored in an airtight tin until needed; do the same with any cut-up pieces of cake that will be sent to friends and relations.

At many American weddings the Bride's cake, which is eaten at the reception, is a decorated sponge cake. The Groom's cake, which is the rich fruit cake we associate with weddings, is often cut into pieces and boxed before the reception; the boxes are placed on the tables, at the edge of the buffet, or on a silver platter at the door, for guests to help themselves as they leave.

Arriving and welcoming

Arriving and welcoming

The way you deal with the arrival of guests at the reception will depend on the size and formality of the reception and the arrangement of the place where you are holding the reception.

If there are lots of guests who came along to the service but who have not been invited to the reception, it is a nice idea to have a small receiving line for them outside the church, to give them a chance to say their good wishes personally. This will also get you into practice for the more extensive one at the reception! The idea of any receiving line is simply to make sure that every guest has the chance to congratulate the couple, wish them well, meet the parents, and thank the hosts of the wedding – whoever they happen to be. Consequently a formal receiving line at a formal reception will include all the people who have been important in the planning of the wedding.

A full line-up for a receiving line will be as follows, in this order: bride's mother, bride's father, groom's mother, groom's father, bride, groom, chief bridesmaid, other attendants. It is generally better not to have small attendants in the receiving line; they will be too small to join in its main purpose, and will quickly become bored. Generally the best man will not be in the receiving line as he is supposed to be the last to leave the church, so that he can be sure that all the guests have been safely despatched to the reception. However, if the receiving line is delayed until all the guests are at the reception venue, the best man could be included next to the groom and before the chief bridesmaid.

1   2   3   4   5   6

At a less formal reception the receiving line could simply consist of the bride's mother, the groom's mother and then the bride and groom. If the wedding is informal, guests can be greeted by the bride and groom on their own. This last arrangement is also often a good idea when relationships are complicated by divorce, step-parents, etc.

At large informal receptions the services of an announcer are sometimes employed, although this is probably rather an affectation unless you are really moving in the highest strata of society! Generally it is sufficient for each guest to make it obvious to the first in the receiving line who he or she is; don't expect everyone to remember you, as all the guests will be out of their normal context and it is easy for minds to go blank when faced with lots of semi-familiar people. The official way to continue the receiving line is for each person involved to present the guest to the next in line with an appropriate remark suited to the depth of their acquaintance – for instance 'James, this is my cousin Peter', or 'Mrs Jones, meet Julie our chief bridesmaid', etc. In fact, the receiving lines these days are likely to be far more spontaneous, and people are unlikely to need hints on what to say to the right people.

If you are having a receiving line you should stay in it until every guest, as far as you can tell, has arrived safely. Once the company seems to be complete, then the meal can be started. If you are having a sit-down meal, the bridal party will make their way to the top table and this will be the signal for the waiters to start serving; everyone else should be in place by this stage. If you are having a buffet, the Master of Ceremonies or the bride's father can loudly invite everyone to begin eating.

7 8

A formal receiving line
1. Bride's mother
2. Bride's father
3. Groom's mother
4. Groom's father
5. Bride
6. Groom
7. Chief bridesmaid
8. Other attendants

Seating

Seating

If you are having a buffet you need to bother very little about seating people in particular places, although you should always make sure that the bridal party has a formal table where they can be served. If you are having a sit-down meal, however, it is important to sort out the seating sensibly so that everyone is in the best position through the meal.

The guests like to be able to see the bridal party in all their splendour, and it is also nice for the newly-married couple to be able to look out over the

---

1 Arrangement for an ordinary wedding

Best man	●
Groom's mother	●
Bride's father	●
BRIDE	●
GROOM	●
Bride's mother	●
Groom's father	●
Chief bridesmaid	●

2 Arrangement when the bride's parents are divorced and both parents have remarried

Bride's stepmother	●
Best man	●
Groom's mother	●
Bride's father	●
BRIDE	●
GROOM	●
Bride's mother	●
Groom's father	●
Chief bridesmaid	●
Bride's stepfather	●

3 Arrangement when the groom's parents are divorced and both parents have remarried

Chief bridesmaid	●
Groom's stepfather	●
Groom's mother	●
Bride's father	●
BRIDE	●
GROOM	●
Bride's mother	●
Groom's father	●
Groom's stepmother	●
Best man	●

4 Arrangement when both sets of parents are divorced and all have remarried

Groom's stepfather	●
Bride's stepmother	●
Best man	●
Groom's mother	●
Bride's father	●
BRIDE	●
GROOM	●
Bride's mother	●
Groom's father	●
Chief bridesmaid	●
Bride's stepfather	●
Groom's stepmother	●

✳✳✳✳✳✳✳✳✳✳ ✳✳✳✳✳✳✳✳✳✳✳✳✳✳✳✳✳✳✳✳✳

reception and see all their friends and relations enjoying themselves, so there should be a top table where the main participants sit. This is generally arranged so that there are people on one side only, facing the rest of the room, and the table may be set on a raised dais or stage if the room has one. The basic top table arrangements for traditional weddings are shown left.

Of course, there are numerous variations within these basic schemes; for instance, if one parent is widowed, and the other set of parents have divorced and only one has remarried. The basic idea is that husbands and wives (or ex-husbands and ex-wives!) should not sit together. If parents have divorced and remarried, their new partners should be at the same end of the table. Bearing these considerations in mind, sort out a sensible arrangement; don't let convention dictate an uncomfortable arrangement, for instance if it would decree sitting two people together who can't stand each other!

If one of the chief participants is missing, for instance, if one of the parents is widowed or if another cannot be present because of illness, fill the gap on the top table with a relative or a close family friend who will be able to take on the appropriate duties of conversation and hospitality.

The top table may be part of a horseshoe shape or E shape, with longer tables butting up to it at right angles; if this is so, the groom's family and friends should be at one end of the arrangement and the bride's at the other. This is simply to make conversation and mixing among the guests easier; if one guest finds that he only knows the groom and he is sitting beside someone who only knows the bride, conversation may be a little difficult to initiate.

If you are having a sit-down meal it is best to plan where everyone is going to sit, even if there are lots of smaller tables dotted around the room. If you do the planning you can make sure that everyone will be sitting near guests they will find congenial, that children are sitting with, or under the watchful eye of, their parents, and that there is a good balance of men and women on each table and through the room in general. You may prefer to have all the children sitting together near one of the doors so that they can disappear to the garden or another room to play when they get bored without too much disruption. Any mothers of small children should also be near the doors so that they can get up without embarrassment to deal with feeding, changing, crying, etc.

Toasts and speeches

Toasts and speeches

The speeches and toasts can be either the highlight or the low point of a wedding reception, depending on the participants!

The purposes of the speeches are twofold; first to congratulate the couple and wish them well in their future life together, and secondly to say thank you to appropriate people. Many people quake when they know that they are going to have to make a speech at a wedding, but if you familiarise yourself with what you want to say and stick to a few basic guidelines you should be fine. If you are really stumped, there are agencies that will write a speech for you or provide you with a selection of jokes, anecdotes or quotations.

✱ ✱ ✱

The bride's father

In this country, the first person to make a speech is usually the bride's father, if he is alive. If he is not, this speech could be made by whoever has given her away, or by an old family friend or favourite uncle or godfather. Generally this speech will say how happy the father is to see his daughter marrying the man of her choice, and how he is sure that all the guests want to join him in wishing the couple well. He may include one or two funny references to events leading up to the wedding, or from her childhood, but this should not be an excuse for causing the bride to squirm with embarrassment over tales of her first boyfriends or her early questions on where babies come from! The bride's father will then propose a toast to the couple; this could take the form of 'the bride and groom!', or 'Andrew and Sheila' (or whatever the couple's names are), or 'to the happy couple!' All the guests should raise their glasses, repeat the toast, and drink to the couple.

The groom

The groom is the next person to speak, and he will do so on behalf of the couple – the assumption being that the bride is too full of maidenly coyness to say anything herself! The groom's speech is usually the one that gives least scope for wit, as his task is mainly to thank people who have been involved in setting up the marriage and reception. He should thank the bride's parents (or whoever else has hosted the reception) for their generosity, and also for providing him with his bride; he should also thank anyone else whose contribution has been outstanding, for instance those who have cooked the food, made the bride's dress, found the new couple a home, etc – or even introduced them in the first place. He then usually makes mention of the

support of the attendants, and proposes a toast to the bridesmaids. If there are lots of bridesmaids the toast can simply be 'the bridesmaids'; if there are only one or two he can toast them by name. Again the guests raise their glasses, repeat the toast and drink.

The best man

Traditionally the best man's speech is the highlight of the reception; somehow it always seems much more permissible to embarrass the groom than it does to embarrass the bride! The best man is officially replying to the toast on behalf of the bridesmaids, but in fact he has the chance to pull the whole proceedings together with style. Anecdotes from the couple's courting days always go down well, provided that they are not too cruel, and if the best man has known the groom for many years there are often chances to let the guests in on various well-kept secrets. When the best man has finished his speech he should read out any telegrams and important cards (having vetted them first for unsavoury remarks . . .). If any guest of importance has been unable to attend the wedding, for instance a brother abroad or a parent in hospital, he may propose a toast to absent friends. At the end of the speeches, or a little while afterwards, the bride and groom cut the cake, and this concludes the official part of the reception.

Tips for making speeches

Do:
make notes in case your mind goes blank
keep it brief – five minutes should be a maximum
try to include a joke or two to lighten the tension
plan what you want to say well in advance
rehearse your speech in the preceding week, to check that you have
  grasped the salient points

Don't:
make embarrassing references to anyone
tell blue jokes
fidget, scratch or put you hand over your mouth
mutter and look down at your feet
sound as though you can't wait to finish!

Going away

Going away

After the formal part of the reception is over, the bride and groom should plan to have a time when they can circulate, separately or together, and talk to all of the guests informally. This may be the only chance that you get to see your guests on an informal level, so make the most of it. If possible this should be done while you are still in all your wedding finery; it will be a chance for the guests to admire your outfits at close quarters as well as to give you their good wishes.

Once you have chatted to all your guests, and at a suitable time chosen in advance, you can retire from the reception to change out of your wedding clothes. Of course it is important to make sure that your going away outfits and any luggage you need for your honeymoon are safely despatched to the reception so that they are there when you need them; this is the kind of task that can be entrusted to a family friend, or it could be left up to the best man to perform this service.

Make sure in advance that your reception venue has a suitable room for you to change in, and where you can leave your wedding clothes safely for your relatives and helpers to pick up and deal with. If your reception is in an hotel, restaurant or club it should be easy for them to provide a suitable room, and of course if you are at home these arrangements are even easier. If the reception is in a church hall, you may find that it is possible to change in the vestry of the church – or there may be a smaller, separate hall or room in the same building. These are all details to check when you book the reception.

Make sure that the people who will be sorting out your wedding clothes know where they now are and what has to be done with them, for instance, whether any cleaning is needed, or whether hired clothes have to be back by a particular date or time. If the clothes are your own, make sure that you tell someone if you have spilt wine, food, ink, etc, on them, so that the stains are not permanently ingrained by the time that you return from honeymoon!

Now is the time for any special or extra farewells; it is a nice gesture for you to go round as a couple and thank privately all the people who have been particularly involved with the wedding preparations and, of course, you will want to say a particular farewell to both sets of parents as you begin your married life. There will probably not be time to go round everyone again, which is why it is important to visit all the guests at the reception. Make sure

✳✳✳✳✳✳✳✳✳✳✳✳✳✳✳✳✳✳✳✳✳✳✳✳✳✳✳✳✳✳

that all your luggage is stowed safely in whatever transport you have chosen, and then if you have a Master of Ceremonies he will announce that you are about to leave. If you don't have anyone to fill this role, make it obvious to the wedding party that you are ready to go and they can encourage the guests to cluster round to bid you a final farewell.

At this stage it is often traditional for the bride to throw her bouquet over her shoulder into the group of guests. Supposedly the person who catches it will be the next one to marry. In olden days the bride often threw one of her wedding shoes for the same purpose, but this has been superseded by the bouquet, probably for safety reasons! At this stage also the couple are often showered with confetti – watch out for the more ruthless guests shoving handfuls down your neck or into your pockets.

Practical jokes frequently rear their heads as the couple leave to go on honeymoon. If you are driving away, hide your car somewhere inaccessible until the last minute if possible to avoid it being daubed with slogans, shaving foam, old boots and toilet rolls. Other traditional tricks such as placing a kipper (presumably chosen because kippers are the smelliest foods available) on the engine of the car can cause great amusement to the guests and great irritation to you! Stones in the hubcaps, tin cans tied to the bumpers and balloons tied to the roof are other traditional decorations for the car of the newly-wed couple. You may prefer to leave your reception in greater style, by horse and carriage, boat or even balloon – or you might play safe and order a taxi!

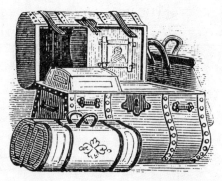

Dealing with presents

Dealing with presents

If you are very lucky, all your guests will have sent their wedding presents in advance by post so that none at all will appear at your wedding reception, but this is becoming less and less common and many guests will probably arrive clutching small or large beribboned parcels.

The first problem is what to do with the presents during the reception. It is very awkward if the couple are handed presents while they are in the receiving line. One solution is to have a special table just inside the door for presents; this way the guests can get rid of their encumbrances early on and are then free to shake hands, take a drink, etc. The first few guests to arrive with presents can be asked to place them on the table, and others arriving later will then see the purpose of the table and follow suit.

Another solution is to have a table elsewhere in the room, perhaps as part of the overall decoration – presents could even be placed around the cake to form a display in themselves. If neither of these ideas proves practical, the

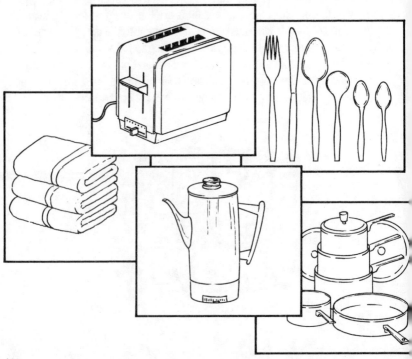

best man, chief bridesmaid or bride's mother can be detailed to take charge of any presents that are handed to the couple and to form a surreptitious pile somewhere out of harm's way.

Every couple's nightmare over presents is when the labels or cards become detached from the presents they were with, so it is a good idea to detail someone to look after this side of things. Perhaps a younger member of the family could be armed with a roll of sellotape and instructed to fix the cards and labels firmly onto the wrappings so that neither goes astray.

The second problem is what to do with the presents when the reception is over. Of course, if you are both staying around for an evening party you can deal with the presents yourselves and take them to an appropriate venue, either your new home or perhaps the bride's mother's house. If you are going straight away on honeymoon then it is best if the best man or bride's mother takes charge of all the presents and looks after them safely until you return from your holiday.

Evening parties

Evening parties

Many couples these days choose to have an evening party for wider groups of friends when they have not been able to invite them all to the reception. This is an ideal opportunity for colleagues, friends from sports teams or clubs, etc, to give you their own good wishes for your married life and also to join in the celebrations.

* * *

The venue for an evening party can be almost anywhere. Since you will probably be doing this in addition to a reception you may want to keep the costs down, so a hired hall will probably be perfect. If you want to do things more formally, perhaps to have a full meal or a formal dance, then again you can hire a room in an hotel or restaurant. Since the evening party is often specifically to entertain the couple's friends, it is appropriate for the couple to offer to pay for it themselves. This need not be an expensive undertaking; you could just provide drinks and snacks, or you could even make it a bring a bottle party.

The style of the party is entirely up to you; choose it to suit your own preferences and the ages and interests of those who will be coming. You can have a disco or other music such as a jazz band, steel band or even orchestra; your local paper will probably give you plenty of ideas for entertainment. The food can be just crisps and peanuts or could be a full buffet or a formal meal. If you wish you could just have an evening celebration in a pub or club, where people could buy their own drinks and just have an excuse to get together and wish you well.

The timing of an evening party can be awkward, particularly if some people have been to the service and then have a gap of several hours to fill before the party. If groups of friends will be attending who all know each other you could suggest that they all go out for tea together, or that another of your friends entertains them informally for the afternoon; then they won't feel too much like lost souls in the intervening time. Whatever kind of party you choose, make sure that it is one that needs the absolute minimum of organisation from you; you will have far too much to think about on the day to be bothered with organising yet another event.

You will need to decide too how much time you are going to spend at the party yourselves. Remember that you will probably be absolutely dropping by this stage; never underestimate the degree of exhaustion you are likely to feel at the end of the day! You may choose just to make a token appearance at the beginning of the party and then let the other guests enjoy themselves while you slip away quietly; this is a very good arrangement if you want to get away to an hotel, etc, the same night, and if you have some responsible people around in whose hands you can leave the rest of the evening's entertainment. On the other hand you may want to be there till the bitter end yourselves – especially if you are planning to spend your first night nearby, so you haven't got far to stagger home! Or you may want to choose a compromise; stay for about half the party and then have your ceremonial 'going away', since you won't have had one at the reception.

Evening parties need not be confined to 'overflow receptions' for those on the fringe of your families. Evening parties in your absence can be a very pleasurable way of entertaining friends and relatives who have travelled from a distance for the wedding and are going to be staying the night in the locality. If you haven't had your reception at home the bride's mother may feel up to holding a small, informal get-together for favourite relatives, and again it is a courteous way to entertain the groom's family if they are staying in a town far from home. If both sets of parents live in your home town then it will be very easy for them to get together and go out for a meal, say, and relax after a busy day, letting someone else do all the hard work. You may even want to pay yourselves for your parents to go out for a meal, as a way of saying thank you for all the effort of the day, and the preparations leading up to it.

Whatever kind of evening party you plan, make sure that there is someone responsible and trustworthy looking after it, and that all the arrangements are quite clear about when to finish, clearing up, paying for hired halls, food, etc. Then there will be no loose ends for bemused friends and relations to try and sort out.

Choosing & planning

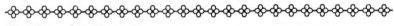

Choosing a honeymoon

Honeymoons used to be a luxury that only the rich could afford, but gradually the custom grew for most couples to take a few days off work, and now a fortnight's honeymoon is fairly standard for most couples. When you are planning your own honeymoon, there are various questions to be taken into consideration.

* * *

Where?

The venue of your honeymoon is, of course, one of the most important details to settle soon in the debate. You will need to talk over your priorities; are you looking for guaranteed sunshine? Good food? A particular sport, such as sailing or climbing or canoeing? A particular interest to follow, such as birdwatching, archaeology or exotic cooking? Do you want to take the opportunity to visit far-off places that you might never have the opportunity to see otherwise?

Fix on your priorities, and then choose a venue that fits in with them. Your honeymoon should be your own personal choice, and you don't need to be influenced by other people's ideas of where is or isn't a suitable place for a honeymoon. Money will, of course, play a huge part in your arrangements; for instance your priority may be hot sunshine, but your budget will dictate whether you find this in Majorca or Hawaii! You will have spent a great deal of money on your wedding, unless you are one of the lucky couples whose parents have footed all the bills, and you don't want to start your married life mortgaged up to the hilt; on the other hand you do want to have a holiday together that you can look back on as a real time of refreshment and enjoyment.

If you are definite about going abroad but need to do so on a strict budget, then you may want to fit in with an ordinary package tour. Venues that are popular for trips from this country, and therefore won't be too expensive in terms of travel and accommodation costs, include the Balearic Islands (Majorca, Ibiza, etc), Malta, Spain and Portugal, France, Greece, Italy, Austria, Switzerland and Germany – and the Channel Islands. Slightly more exotic destinations include North America, South America, Turkey, Yugoslavia, Sweden, Norway, Holland, Belgium, Canada, Finland, Corsica and North Africa.

If money really isn't a problem – lucky you! Your options are numerous, and you will be able to choose a destination that others may only dream of. Your

options could include exotic islands such as Bali, the Cayman Islands, the Seychelles, Trinidad and Tobago, the Maldives or the Virgin Islands. Other choices could be such places as India, China, Singapore, Hong Kong, Sri Lanka, etc.

Of course you don't need to go abroad – especially if the forecast is for good weather over here. There are many very attractive parts of the British Isles, and numerous pretty places to stay when you are there, but costs can mount up for the very picturesque venues. Nevertheless if your main priority is not sun, but something such as fell walking, pony trekking, sightseeing, etc, a honeymoon in this country may well be your best bet.

How long?

The length of your honeymoon will generally be dictated by two factors: work and money. Work may well restrict the time you have off, specific days you have to be back for meetings, etc, and when exactly you can take your honeymoon. Your budget will dictate some of your options, although there should be some flexibility even on the smallest budget. For instance, you may find that for the price of staying in an hotel in this country you could go abroad on a package trip for the same amount of time or could go self-catering for twice as long. Conversely you might decide that instead of going on a package trip for a fortnight to Ibiza, you would rather have a luxury 5-day trip to Morocco. Hunt around for the best bargains, and the type of trip that fits into your own ideas of what you want from your honeymoon.

Economy

Even if your budget is very limited, it may still be possible for you to have several weeks away together at the start of your marriage. For instance, you may have a friend or a colleague who has a holiday home you could borrow free of charge. Many travel firms do special honeymoon packages or bargain breaks for couples trying to economise. You may also find that if you take your honeymoon at particular times of the year you can fit in with the offpeak seasons. Other ways of economising are to go camping (not everyone's idea of a honeymoon!) or caravanning, to book in at a bed and breakfast guest house rather than an expensive hotel, or to choose a self-catering cottage or holiday flat. If you are determined to stay in an hotel, you can economise on their honeymoon suites which may well be very expensive; either book into an ordinary room, or book the honeymoon suite for a night or two and then a less expensive room for the rest of the stay.

Choosing and planning – Going-away clothes

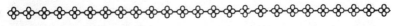

Going-away clothes

You will need to choose a practical set of clothes to change into after the formal part of the wedding reception is over; many women buy a special outfit so that they can still feel that they are celebrating a new life. Choose clothes that will be comfortable and crease resistant, especially if you will be travelling for quite a distance after the reception. Make sure that your outfit can be adapted for all kinds of weathers, for instance that you have a jacket, shawl or cardigan that can be worn or carried as the weather demands. Shown here are some ideal going-away outfits that could be adapted to suit your own needs and tastes.

Travel arrangements

Travel arrangements

Your travel arrangements will need to be very carefully thought out, especially if you have a specific plane, train or boat that you need to catch after the reception. Be realistic about the time that you will be able to get away from the reception, and also make realistic assessments of how long it will take you to get to your destination, remembering that you will both be tired.

Many couples choose to spend their first night in an hotel in this country even if they are going abroad the next day – this can be an ideal way of recovering from the exhaustion of the day itself without having to cope in a foreign country as well. Many airports have hotels near them, and some of the hotels even have bridal suites so that you can really spend your first night in style. The hotels may not be in very attractive settings, but all you are likely to want the first night is a good dinner and a comfortable bed!

If you will be driving away from the reception, don't forget that your car is likely to be decorated in various appropriate ways. If this idea appals you, make sure that your car is well hidden and arrange for a trusted friend to drive you to its hiding place when you are ready. If you don't mind having the car decorated, remember to allow some time in your timetable for stopping at a friendly garage and repairing the damage.

Alternatively, you may choose to leave your reception by taxi, or a friend could drive you to the station, car hire firm, etc. Whatever your travel arrangements are, double check them before the day itself and again on the morning of the wedding day; this could be a task that you could ask your best man to undertake. If you are using your own car, make sure that it is well supplied with petrol, oil and water, and that the tyres are pumped up.

You may choose to leave your reception by some more exotic means, such as a carriage and pair, a boat, or even a balloon! You could also arrange for the wedding car that brought you from the service to return and see you off to your honeymoon in real style. Confetti will probably be liberally sprinkled at this stage, so check your pockets, collars, etc, unless you want everyone to know that you are newlyweds!

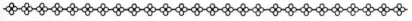

Checklist for planning your honeymoon

Where will we go?	Will someone have supplies of food, milk, etc, ready when we return?
How long will the holiday last?	What tour operator are we travelling with?
Will we be touring or staying in one place?	Who is our contact in case of difficulties?
What date will we leave?	Is there a phone number or address where we can be reached?
Do we want to stay anywhere different the first night?	Will we need any extra money for accommodation, petrol, tips, etc?
If so, where?	Will we need money for meals?
What date will we return?	Will we need extra money for sightseeing trips?
What transport will we need from the reception?	How much spending money will we need?
What time will we need to leave the reception?	How will we take this – currency, traveller's cheques, etc?
Do we need to hire a car?	Do we need foreign currency?
If so, when and where will we pick it up?	If so, when do we pick it up?
Do we want to take our car abroad with us?	Do we need visas for the country we're visiting?
If so, what documents are needed?	Do we need any injections?
	Do we both have current passports?
What are the times of our travel arrangements on the outward journey?	Do we both have suitable going-away outfits?
What are the times of our travel arrangements home?	Does the bride's passport need her name changed?

Packing

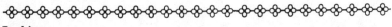

Packing

It's easy to neglect preparations for your honeymoon in the rush of preparations for the wedding day itself, but most of your packing can be done well in advance, with just the addition of last-minute things such as washing kits and money at the end. While there is plenty of time, think out carefully the kind of things you will need and begin assembling them, and this will save you a lot of headaches when the pressure is on.

* * *

Clothes

Choose clothes that are suitable for the climate of the place you will be visiting. Most people take far more clothes than they need when they go abroad; it's horrifying how quickly they can mount up and make your suitcase feel as if it weighs a ton. Find out about the place that you will be staying; are you going to a self-catering place in the sun, in which case you will probably want only swimsuits, shorts and T-shirts and sundresses, with the occasional more elegant outfit, or are you going to an upmarket hotel where you will be expected to dress for dinner? Will you need long jeans or long-sleeved shirts to protect you from insects, sunburn, rough rides on camels or donkeys? Is there any special clothing you will need, for instance if you plan to do a lot of sailing, climbing, canoeing, etc?

Equipment

Find out as much as you can about the facilities of the hotel or guest house where you will be staying – for instance, it would be annoying to cart a hairdryer and travel iron several thousand miles only to discover that every room has their own provided. If you will be self-catering, do you need to take food with you or can it be bought nearby? If you are going on a special interest holiday, is there any equipment that you need to take with you? If so, add it to your list and collect it early on so that you aren't scrabbling around trying to obtain it at the last minute.

Documents

Your documents will of course be the most important items of all; if you forget a swimsuit or underclothes it will be annoying but not disastrous as you can always buy replacements, but if you forget your passports or plane tickets you may not be able to travel at all. Insurance is vitally important too; no-one wants to think of disasters happening on their honeymoon, but if they do it would at least be nice to have insurance cover for them. Make a list of all the documents you will need, and double-check it the day of the wedding.

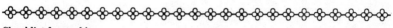

Checklist for packing

☐	Informal clothes	☐	Timetables
☐	Formal clothes	☐	Maps
☐	Swimsuits	☐	Plane, train or boat tickets
☐	Nightclothes	☐	Passports
☐	Underwear	☐	Visas
☐	Jackets and coats	☐	Travel sickness tablets
☐	Dressing gown	☐	Basic first aid kit
☐	Jewellery	☐	Car documents
☐	Shoes	☐	Driving licences
☐	Washing kits	☐	Foreign currency
☐	Shampoo, conditioner, hairdryer, etc	☐	Travellers' cheques, etc
☐	Contraception	☐	Address of hotel or guest house
☐	Make-up	☐	Contact number in case of difficulties
☐	Guidebooks	☐	Insurance documents

How will our bags get to the reception?

How will we get to the hotel/station/airport?

Where will you live?

ⵣⵣⵣⵣⵣⵣⵣⵣⵣⵣⵣⵣⵣⵣⵣⵣⵣⵣⵣⵣⵣⵣⵣⵣⵣ

Where will you live?

One extremely important question to decide well before the wedding day is where you will live after you are married. If one of you already has a house it may be easiest to move in together there; however, the place may not be big enough, particularly if it is a typical single person's flat or bedsit, so this may not be practical. Or, you may be setting up your married life in a completely new area, and may have to find new accommodation from scratch.

* * *

Living with relatives

If you are not well off you may decide to live with one or other sets of parents, or with another relative, until you can afford a place of your own. This, like most living arrangements, has both advantages and disadvantages. The advantages are that you don't need to get involved in the trouble and expense of buying a house until you have had a chance to adjust to married life; you will be able to live more cheaply than if you were living on your own; you should be able to share some of the chores such as cooking, washing, cleaning, gardening, shopping, etc; and both couples will have someone else around for companionship. Potential problems are, of course, manifold, and this situation may be particularly difficult for the son or daughter-in-law who has married into the family; he or she may feel that they have not taken on a marriage partner but a whole family!

If you are going to live in this kind of arrangement when you are first married, talk it over all together and make sure that *everyone* is happy with it. Make clear certain conditions so that there will be no misunderstanding – for instance, exactly how much you are going to pay for housekeeping, how the chores will be divided, how you will pay for electricity, phone calls, laundry, etc. If at all possible, set a definite time limit on the arrangement – for instance that you will live there for a year while you save, and then start looking for a place of your own. Some families are able to make over a whole part of their house into a flat or annexe for the newly-married couple, which can mean that you have a lot of the advantages of living under one roof without many of the disadvantages.

Be sensible and realistic about how the arrangement is likely to work; for instance if you find it difficult to get on with one set of parents, it will be a very difficult start to your married life if you are constantly quarrelling. If it is your parents that you will be living with, be sensitive to the fact that your husband or wife will probably feel very left out at first as the newcomer to the home.

House-sharing

Sharing a home with friends has many of the advantages and potential
disadvantages of living with relatives, but if you choose to live with friends you
can at least ensure that you have similar tastes, interests and lifestyles. If you
are looking at this kind of arrangement, make sure that *all* of you get on well
together, that there is no danger of sexual tensions or jealousies among you,
and that you are all able to communicate well if you are unhappy with any
aspect of your living arrangements. Once again, make it clear at the outset
what each person will be expected to contribute in terms of money, time and
talents.

Renting accommodation

Renting accommodation on your own can be a good half-way stage between
leaving home and buying a house of your own; you will have independence and
the chance to be together without the extra financial strains of owning and
caring for your own house and having to make decisions on the rates,
maintenance, etc. Of course not all renting is plain sailing. If you are renting a
council house the conditions will be well laid out and your duties clearly
detailed; the council will pay for the maintenance of the property and you will
simply need to keep it in good order.

If you are renting privately, try to build up a good relationship with your
landlord as he will be the key to whether you are happy in that flat or house.
If possible, try and find out about the landlord before you make any firm
arrangements, for instance, from other people in the same block of flats or in
other properties administered by the same landlord. Find out whether he is
helpful, difficult over money, co-operative over repairs, etc; also find out how
often the rent has to be paid, whether a cheque or cash is preferred, whether
this includes heating, lighting, gas, water, phone, etc.

It is also worthwhile checking on your rights as a tenant – unfortunately there
are still some unscrupulous landlords around who may try to push you out with
little notice, or put the rent up astronomically as soon as you are settled in. If
the rent is not too high, renting accommodation can give you a good chance to
save capital so that you can put a significant deposit on a house of your own,
which is in turn a good way of reducing your mortgage payments, so although
renting may be a little awkward at times it can be very useful for the
newly-married couple.

Where will you live? – Your own home

Buying a house

These days more and more young couples are buying their own homes either before or when they get married, and many building firms are producing small homes that are an ideal size for young married couples who don't want too much space or garden to look after. A home of your own will give you a foothold in the property market as well as providing a place that feels as though it is truly yours, but of course it is also an expensive business.

***

The mortgage will be your main consideration, as you will have to continue to pay it (or its successor!) for 20–25 years. Mortgages can be obtained from building societies, banks and some other institutions; the companies have cycles when they have either a lot or a little money to lend, and even if you don't manage to get a mortgage as soon as you apply you may find that things alter in the space of a few months or even weeks. Some societies will give 100% mortgages to first-time buyers; others will require a deposit of around 10% and will allow the rest on mortgage. At this point generous parents sometimes make a donation or a loan of some capital to start the new couple off, which can be a great boon and mean the difference between a realistic mortgage and a crippling one.

Legal fees are another expense entailed in house-buying; these will include solicitors' fees, search fees, the cost of a survey by the building society and/or your private surveyor, land registry fees, and possibly stamp duty. In addition you will have to pay the costs of any removals of furniture, etc, to the new house, although if you do not already own a great deal this can probably be done yourselves with a self-hire van.

The cost of setting up a home from scratch can be considerable; don't fall into the temptation of buying everything new immediately, but buy second-hand to begin with, or wait a little for your new kitchen units, wall-to-wall carpets, etc. You will find that you can actually get by on very little first of all, and can add to your collection slowly. The worst favour you can do yourselves at the outset of your marriage is to be up to your necks in HP repayments, which have a nasty habit of keeping ahead of the income coming in.

Whatever living arrangements you choose, remember that you are setting up a home for yourselves; it is not your material possessions that are important, but the atmosphere you create around you for your marriage and for people who come to visit you.

New home customs

We're all familiar with the tradition of carrying the new bride across the threshold, but this is only one of many customs the world over for welcoming the newly married couple into their home.

———*———

In Greece the mother gives the bride a glass of honey and water as she enters her own house for the first time, and sometimes the groom's foot has to crush a pomegranate.

In Montenegro the couple are presented with sweet basil, presumably in the hope that their marriage will be equally fragrant.

In one part of Sumatra the bride and groom have to take an imitation siesta together in the village square to show that they are man and wife.

In North Africa the bridegroom's mother throws handfuls of dried fruit over the new couple, and also breaks an egg on the forehead of the mare or mule delivering the wife to her new home.

In some South American countries a new wing is added to the bride's family's home each time a daughter married – with the result that some of the houses become very large.

In some West African tribes the bride takes up her wifely duties ceremoniously, one by one, as she enters the new house. First she sweeps out the hut, then fetches water, prepares a meal and grinds corn. When her mother-in-law considers that she is sufficiently proficient in these tasks, she instructs the bride to place a pot of beer in the hut as an invitation to the groom to join her.

In one Central Asian tribe the bride and groom do not live together at first. She busies herself preparing their new aquoi, or felt tent, and its furnishings; during this time the groom visits her secretly once a week. When the tent is finished the groom arrives ceremoniously to carry off the bride and his new home.

In Greece the bride is traditionally accompanied to her new home by flute players, both mothers, and a procession of torchbearers.

Thankyous

Thankyous

When you return from honeymoon there will be lots to sort out, but don't neglect any extra thankyous that are needed. Of course there will probably be quite a few thankyou notes for wedding presents that arrived on the day itself and couldn't be incorporated into the pre-wedding arrangements, but there may also be some people to whom you want to say a special thank you. For instance, it will be nice for both sets of parents to have a written appreciation of their help and support through the hectic wedding plans and on the day; you might even care to send a bouquet or a little present to them. It will also be nice for your bridesmaids, best man and any other attendants to receive a written thankyou. For all these people it will be nice to have a good enlargement of one of your best wedding photographs, perhaps in a special frame, for them to put in a position of prominence!

There will probably also be other people you will want to thank formally – caterers, photographs, flower arrangers, people who helped at an evening party, car drivers, ushers, people from work who clubbed together for a special present, etc. It will make everyone feel that their hard work was appreciated if you can find the time to drop them a note or make a quick telephone call.

People we need to say thankyou to	Phone call or letter?	Done (date)

People we need to say thankyou to	Phone call or letter?	Done (date)

Letting people know

Letting people know

Of course everyone who came to your wedding will know that you are well and truly married, but some of your more distant friends and relations may not. Also, even your wedding guests may not know your new address and telephone number. So it's worth making a list and working through it methodically to ensure that everyone is covered. In addition you will need to inform any clubs, professional organisations, banks, etc, of your change of address (and possibly of name also).

	Date done
Bank	
Insurance companies	
Building society	
Premium bonds	
Car insurance company	
Work	
Garage	
Doctor	
Dentist	
Book clubs	
Mail order catalogues	
Clubs and associations	
Other firms or organisations	

Relatives	Date done

Friends	Date done

Money

Money

Spending can be one of the biggest sources of contention within a marriage, and this can be especially true when things are very tight after an expensive wedding and honeymoon, often combined with the cost of setting up a new home as well. It's important to sort out your priorities and expenditures early on, especially if you have used up all your savings on the wedding and house, to make sure that you don't get into deep water and place an unnecessary strain on your marriage.

* * *

Bank accounts

You will need to decide whether you are going to have two bank accounts or a joint one. A joint bank account may make it easier for you to keep track of your money as you will only have to check one set of bank statements; on the other hand separate accounts may be easier for some lifestyles, with each of you taking responsibility for different financial obligations such as the mortgage, housekeeping, bills, entertainments, etc.

Building societies

Once again you may have to decide whether to combine an account or maintain two separate ones; you may choose to keep a building society account as your main means of saving, for instance for special items such as holidays or for a deposit on a house or a car.

Insurance

You may already be covered for personal insurance under your mortgage arrangement, but if not it could be a good time to arrange for life insurance in one another's favour; if you are depending on two incomes and one of these is suddenly curtailed the other partner could be left in great financial difficulties.

Pensions

You may be involved in a pension scheme at work, but if not, or if it is only minimal, your marriage could be the ideal opportunity to take out an easy saving plan spread over the maximum number of years. You may also want to start saving towards the cost of having children, schooling, etc.

It is well worthwhile making out a simple budget for your first year, and then revising it each year as your circumstances change, so that you have rough guidelines to keep to and will be able to assess what you can and can't afford realistically. Use this page to plan your rough incomings and outgoings, and see if they tally – if not, some adjustments will have to be made!

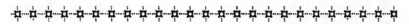

Incomings	£ per year
Husband's income	
Wife's income	
Interest, etc	
Any other incomings	
Total	

Outgoings	£ per year
Mortgage or rent	
Insurance	
Community charge	
Gas	
Electricity	
Phone	
Housekeeping	
HP payments or bank loan repayments	
Things for the house	
Holidays	
Clothes	
Presents	
Entertainment	
Travelling expenses	
Car payments, insurance, tax	
Car maintenance	
House maintenance	
Sport	
Extras, eg. haircuts, dental fees, prescription charges, club memberships, magazines and books, records and tapes	
Total	

Remembering the day

Remembering the day

Of course you will have your photographs, and possibly a video film, of all stages of the wedding and reception, both formal and informal, to help you capture the flavour of every moment of your wedding day. However, there are also plenty of other ways of helping you remember the things that made the day special – the details of the preparations, the goodwill messages of your guests, scraps of fabric from the bride's and bridesmaids' gowns, and flowers from your bouquets.

* * *

Keepsake books

These books can be bought ready prepared with boxes for you to fill in with all the details of your wedding – who the bridesmaids were, what the bride's mother wore, what flowers were in the bouquets, etc – or you could make your own from a large scrapbook or blank photo album. In this you can include scraps of the relevant fabrics, planning sketches of the dresses and colour schemes, photos of the church flowers, drawings of your church, details of any disasters, pictures of the cake, a few dried flowers from your bouquet, etc, samples of your wedding stationery – anything that helps evoke the atmosphere of the day and all the preparations for it.

Guest books

Once again, you can either buy one of these specially printed, or can make your own and circulate it during the wedding reception. Each page will have a few boxes or sections where each guest can write a goodwill message – serious or silly – for the newly married couple. In years to come you will be able to browse through the album and recall the day even more clearly.

Embroidered samplers

One very lovely way to remember your wedding day is by embroidering a sampler. This doesn't need to be very complicated; its complexity can be decided by your sewing skills! Kits can be bought that provide a pattern for the outside borders and decorations and then alphabet instructions so that you can include your own names and the date, or you could design your own sampler from scratch and incorporate details that are particularly relevant to you, for instance including a monogram, or embroidering some of the flowers that were in your bouquet.

-ᵼ-

Flower collages

Fresh flowers are wonderful on the day itself, but inevitably they soon lose
their bloom and scent. However, it is possible to have your flowers preserved
in various ways so that you still have a vivid reminder of their beauty. Many
firms these days will make a collage from dried blooms from your bouquet,
perhaps including a small cameo wedding picture or mounting the collage on a
piece of the same fabric as your wedding dress. Or you can dry your bouquet
yourself by placing it in a shoebox full of silica gel crystals and leaving it until
all the moisture has been absorbed by the crystals. Alternatively you could
have a replica made in silk flowers of your wedding bouquet, which would
capture the colours without the problem of dealing with fresh flowers.

1 A dried flower collage
2 A replica of a wedding bouquet in silk

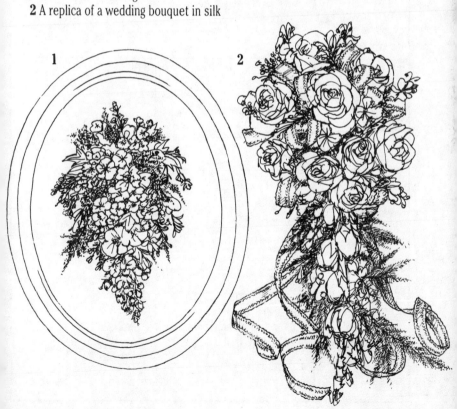

Remembering the day – Anniversaries

Anniversaries

Of course one of the best ways of remembering your wedding day is to celebrate your wedding anniversaries as they come along. Use this day to recall all the good things about your marriage – past and present – and to

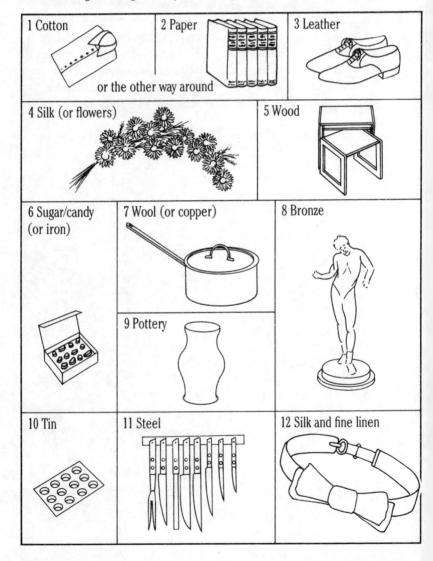

1 Cotton

2 Paper

or the other way around

3 Leather

4 Silk (or flowers)

5 Wood

6 Sugar/candy (or iron)

7 Wool (or copper)

8 Bronze

9 Pottery

10 Tin

11 Steel

12 Silk and fine linen

reassess it and take stock of your relationship to prepare for the year ahead. Each wedding anniversary has a specific title – chosen traditionally to replace the wedding gifts that would have worn out by that particular year! You might want to choose an appropriate gift for each other for each one.

13 Lace	14 Ivory
15 Crystal	20 China
25 Silver	30 Pearl	35 Coral	40 Ruby
45 Sapphire	50 Gold
55 Emerald	60 or 75 Diamond

Timetables

Timetables

As well as keeping checklists of all the details of your wedding plans, you will need an overall timetable of what to do when, so that everything is planned in good time and nothing gets forgotten. Sort out all the big questions first – date and time, venue of service and reception – then move onto the smaller details once you have worked out the basic framework.

* * *

5–6 months before your wedding you will need to decide when and where you are going to get married, and book up the church or registry office, minister or registrar, reception and caterers. You will also need to book a photographer, someone to video the proceedings, cars and other transport to the service and reception and away from the reception. This is especially important to arrange early if you are getting married in the summer, when many professional firms are booked solid months in advance. Decide where you are going for your honeymoon and make all the necessary travel arrangements. Decide also where you are going to live; if you will be buying a place of your own start looking immediately and try to get the purchase sorted out as soon as possible. Decide on who you want to take part in your wedding, such as best man, bridesmaids, ushers and other attendants, and check that your chosen date is available for them.

*

3–4 months before your wedding start refining some of the details. Decide on what you are both going to wear, and if possible obtain the outfits well in advance. Choose clothes for the attendants as well and buy them or make arrangements for hiring or having them made up in good time for the big day. Plan and order your wedding stationery – this will also involve settling the details of your order of service so that these can be printed. Choose the food and wine for your reception, and detail people to help if you will be doing your own catering or having it done by friends. Order the cake or make it yourself; the taste will be all the better for having matured for a few months. Book a venue for an evening party if you are having one, and any entertainment that will be needed there or at the reception. Choose your flowers for the bride, bridesmaids, church and reception, and buttonholes; discuss these with the florist and order them well in advance. If you haven't yet got your wedding rings, now is the time to buy them. Visit your family planning clinic if necessary.

*

2 months before your wedding, compile a guest list and send out the invitations, and also a gift list if you will be circulating one to all the guests.

Check the final details of banns, service, fees, bellringing, choir, etc, with the minister or registrar, and ensure that everything is arranged on the music side. Choose presents for your attendants and buy or make them, and look for going-away outfits for both of you. Obtain your marriage licence. Finalise plans for your honeymoon and new house. See whether any of your guests will need accommodation, and if so arrange it for them. Plan pre-wedding parties for bride and groom if you are having them.

*

1 month before your wedding check the fit of clothes for yourselves and attendants so that there is time for any adjustments. Visit your hairdresser with your headdress and plan your hairstyle; book up an appointment on the day if necessary. Book any beauty treatments you will be having. Tell the caterers the exact number of guests you will be having, and buy cakeboxes if you will need them for sending wedding cake to people who couldn't attend. Order currency, travellers' cheques, etc, for your honeymoon, and ensure that you both have valid passports. If not, obtain visitors' versions! Inform banks, building societies, clubs, professional organisations, etc, of your change of address and marital status – and name, for the bride. Submit an announcement to the local paper if you want them to carry the news of your wedding. Write as many thankyou notes for presents as possible.

*

The week before your wedding check over all the arrangements for catering, cake, photographs, video, travelling, honeymoon, etc. Pack your cases for your honeymoon and check all your documents. Double-check arrangements with florists and hairdressers, and with car-hire firms. Ensure that you have your orders of service, any hired clothes, etc, ready. Arrange for someone to have supplies of tea, coffee, milk, bread, etc, in your new house when you return. Have a wedding rehearsal and any pre-wedding parties you have planned. Attend your beauty salon, etc, so that you look your best on the day.

*

The day before your wedding double-check all your arrangements. Look at clothes, accessories, honeymoon packing, documents for wedding and honeymoon, orders of service, cake, catering, flowers, hairdressing appointments, transport, rings, foreign currency, passports, marriage licence, etc. Then relax with a good book or take a long walk!

* * *

Timetables – Personal planner

Personal planner

Use these pages to plan the lead-up to your own wedding; fill in the arrangements you need to make, and tick them off as they are done.

5–6 months before the wedding: months .... and ....

3–4 months before the wedding: months .... and ....

2 months before the wedding: month ....

❖❖❖❖❖❖❖❖❖❖❖❖❖❖❖❖❖❖❖❖❖❖❖❖❖❖

1 month before the wedding: month ....

1 week before the wedding: dates ....

Day before the wedding: date ....

Index